V.E.A.R TOWARD

SUCCESS

How you too can apply

Vision, Energy, Attitude and

Resolve to achieve every one

of your dreams!

Contents

Acknowledgements

First and foremost I need to thank my wife, Monique, for her ongoing support and belief in me. When I first brought her to see "the Ark" it was in pretty rough shape. There was no back wall to the building, ratty blue tarps hung in the garage entrances, only a few windows had been installed (and many of them were broken), there was trash, garbage and debris in every room, mouse/squirrel/raccoon poop in every corner, a broken down City of Ottawa bus in the backyard, and heaps of rotting lumber everywhere... It wasn't a pretty picture.

Yet still I said, "So how do you like our new home?"

It took an extremely inspired person to share this Vision I had conjured in my mind. I don't want to give away the story here, but not many women would have the patience to live 2 winters in a Canadian "home" with no heat or running water. There were definitely days when I questioned this undertaking myself. "What had I done? What was I thinking?"

Luckily, Monique was there to answer those questions and remind me of the Vision she and I both shared. Without her, the Ark would never have been completed nor this book ever written.

I also want to thank the friends and family who stopped by to help out with this or that from time to time. Most specifically, I want to thank my friends Al Ritchie, Paul Normore and Nils Meyer. Although I was alone for 95% of the Ark's building process, getting some help from these fellas during that remaining 5% was crucial. Al was there to lend a hand regardless of how mundane and monotonous the project was. Paul always brought with him high energy, enthusiasm and laughter. And with Nils being a master carpenter, his advice on how to turn a rickety structure like the Ark into a sound home was invaluable.

Specifically for the completion of this book I need to thank Steve Hay and Wendy Martel. Steve is one of my oldest friends in Ottawa and is one of the region's foremost graphic designers. It was he who designed the cover for this book. I think he did a great job, I'm just a little disappointed he couldn't make me look any prettier! But he is a graphic designer after all, not God!

I actually just met Wendy at a Running Room motivational talk I did earlier this year, but we hit it off immediately. We both have similar quirky senses of humour, but luckily her grammar is much better than mine. Her assistance in editing this book is very greatly appreciated.

Additionally, I want to thank all those people who have always said I couldn't do it. There were those who said I couldn't work in France without being able to speak French, those who said there was no future for me if I moved to the USA, and there were those that said I couldn't build a house with no training or experience in carpentry, electrical, plumbing, heating, finishing, etc.

Without all of you giving me the opportunity to prove you wrong, I may never have even been motivated to try.

And last, but not least I want to thank all the banks, law firms and insurance companies of the world. 80% of the problems in my life are probably initiated by one of the three above institutions. If it weren't for these folks, books and concepts like V.E.A.R. probably wouldn't be required. We'd all simply be happy and content without even trying!

Thanks to all of you.

About this Book

V.E.AR. Toward Success is a book written not only to motivate you but show you that by simply applying Vision, Energy, Attitude and Resolve you can achieve each and every one of your dreams. Regardless of what they are! This process or philosophy works in the arenas of: career, fitness, finances, relationships, carpentry, whatever...

This book is not only educational, it is also somewhat autobiographical. Coming from a science background, I need proof to support any theories that I read about. Using experiences from my life, I have endeavored to provide real life examples of how I have used Vision, Energy, Attitude, and Resolve to not only achieve success in my mission to build the Ark, but to find happiness in all aspects of my life.

The book concludes with suggestions and a "workbook" for how you too can apply V.E.A.R. to reach your goals and achieve success in each and every arena of your world.

Good luck, have fun, and enjoy the journey.

Background

Hello, my name is Mike Caldwell and I am a self professed goals junkie. I wouldn't say I'm never happy with what I have or what I've accomplished, quite the contrary. I have always been very grateful and appreciative for what my life has provided me. But being somewhat of an adventurer, I'm always looking for that next challenge, and am never content to simply maintain the status quo. There are always new goals, new challenges and different arenas in which to test the waters.

I'm not a self-made millionaire (well not yet anyway), I'm not a cancer survivor, nor have I had to turn my life around after a prolonged stint in prison. I'm just an average guy with average intelligence and an average start in life. But staying "average" has never really appealed to me. I always wanted to do things people said I was crazy for even considering. These choices have proven very stressful for my parents. Even at 39 years old, my parents still request I tell them about things AFTER I have attempted them. They really don't want to know about the things I am planning to do!

....

My mom started dating my dad when she was in grade 8 and he was in grade 9. My dad got his first part-time job in high school working for a corrugated box company. Upon graduating from school, they offered him a full time position. My mom and dad married shortly after graduation and have been happily married ever since. Two years ago my father retired from the only company he has ever worked for.

Life doesn't get much more stable and conservative than that! Don't get me wrong, I'm not knocking the way my parents chose to live their lives. In fact I think it's amazing! They are still very much in love today and they have always been happy. So they have been in love and happy their whole lives! What else could anybody ask for?

Growing up I always had food on the table and clothes on my back. Everything I ever needed was provided for me. We lived in a nice and clean middle class home and we always had a relatively new and meticulously clean middle class car. My family life made "the Cleavers" look like a strung out, hippie family! We were the textbook definition of conservative.

When I told my parents I wanted to go to university to study biology they were completely confused and bewildered. Why did I want to do that? Was a degree in biology going to get me a job? What exactly was I planning to do with my life anyway and how was I expecting to pay for this education? I didn't have answers to any of these questions. I wasn't worried about tomorrow, it wasn't even here yet!

....

So off to university I went. I studied hard in grade 13 and graduated with the third highest average in my class; much to the surprise of most of my teachers. I had just barely passed many of my classes in grades 9 through 11 and, due to arrogance and insubordination; I had been kicked out of my grade 13 English class entirely. But Trent University didn't care about "ancient history" and offered me a full one year scholarship. With this scholarship, and a little bit of money I made as a lifeguard, I had no trouble paying for my first year of school.

In my first summer as a university student my dad was able to get me a job in the factory for the company he worked for. I worked on "the waxer" and my job was to catch hot sheets of cardboard as they passed through the machine that dripped hot wax all over them. Intellectually this wasn't the world's most stimulating job, but I was a union employee and the pay was pretty darn good! In fact, I was earning as much as my dad was in the office and he had been with the company for twenty years already. My dad thought I was nuts when I told him I was quitting such a high paying job just to go back to school.

In my second year I transferred to the University of Guelph. They had a Wildlife Biology degree and courses that I thought might interest me more. But although I thought I was interested in biology, I was really only interested in wolves and backcountry camping! The Citric Acid Cycle, paramecium, basidiomycota, and Mendelson's pea experiments were of very little interest to me. But I survived the year and in my second summer I landed a job as a whitewater raft guide on the Ottawa River. Now this was more like it! THIS was living! Rafting big waves and joking and playing with sexy girls in their bathing suits all day, kayaking and partying all evening... What wasn't there to love?

Descending into "Phil's Hole" on the Ottawa River.

September and the return of school, that's what! After a summer of such fun and freedom, the tedium of academics was suffocating. Why did I care what stage of its lifecycle that red dot under the microscope was in? How was that information ever going to help me?

So after two and a half years of study I decided to drop out! I wasn't planning on quitting school entirely, but I had reached the conclusion that a bachelor's degree in biology certainly wasn't going to land me a job, let alone the career of my dreams. I finished that semester and the following summer I headed up to the Canadian Arctic to work as a raft guide on the Coppermine River. Sure the Ottawa River had been fun, but I had already been there and done that. The Coppermine was an opportunity to travel and explore a whole new world.

This job also gave me an entirely new level of responsibility. On the Ottawa River, my only job was to get the raft down the river safely and ensure the pretty girls in the bikinis had a good time. On the Coppermine, my trips were 14 days long instead of just an afternoon. I was completely responsible for my guests. I had to assist them in setting up their tents and choosing their clothes. I had to fish for them, cook for them and clean up after them. And I had to ensure we traveled the river safely and nobody ventured too far outside of their comfort zone. If someone became sick or injured, I was the ambulance, nurse, and doctor all rolled up in one! I was no longer a kid at a summer-long party; rather I was a guide who was entrusted with the lives of our clients.

Mike Caldwell

Running the Rapids of Rocky Defile on the Coppermine River of
Canada's Northwest Territories

I learned a lot about myself on the Coppermine and that following September I found myself out of Guelph University and attending Niagara College to become an ambulance attendant. From my perspective, working on an ambulance would provide me with unique challenges and diversity and also give me that feeling of satisfaction I experienced being so utterly responsible for people in the Arctic. However, although working on an ambulance could be a great career, it still wasn't the final plan I had for my life. Instead I hoped to use that training as a vehicle for opening other doors and opportunities. As a part time ambulance attendant I was making a decent wage and had the freedom to choose whether I wanted to work my 12 hour shifts during the day or night or on weekends or weekdays. This was a perfect part time job for a university student, so I returned to Guelph to resume my studies.

I knew I wanted to continue rafting that next summer but I had some choices to make. Did I want to continue with the day trips, the partying and the girls, or did I want to return to the more mature and exotic environs of the Canadian Arctic. As this story unfolds you'll learn that when given two choices I always go with the THIRD option. Using the contacts I had made rafting the two previous summers, in 1991 I left Canada to secure a job working as a raft guide and safety kayaker on the Ubaye River, just north of Nice in the French Alps.

Did I know how to speak French? Well, no. Had I ever rafted or kayaked a low-volume, glacially fed, technical mountain river before? Well not exactly... Were these petty concerns going to stop me from being paid to travel Europe? Heck no! I knew what I wanted and was confident that I could learn everything I needed to know long before I was in a position to put anybody's life in danger.

And sure enough, within a couple of weeks I was fluent in "river French". I knew how to say "left", "right", "helmet", "after the bridge" and "paddle or die" en français. What more did I really need to know? The only person who nearly died that summer was me. Twice!

When somebody travels from another country to work in a particular field, it's quite often assumed that they left their native land because there were no challenges left for them there. Although this wasn't the case with me, my fellow French raft guides still assumed I was one of Canada's best. They would frequently say things to me (in French) as a joke, and since I didn't know any better I would naively assume they were being serious and take them up on their offer! This is why 16 years later I am still the only person to ever attempt paddling the Ubaye River in flood in a "hotdog" and the only person to paddle the Bachelot Creek in a full-sized kayak. Both of these ridiculous stunts resulted in near death experiences for me.

But I did survive my time in France and returned to Canada with surprisingly little additional wisdom. I just had one semester to complete at Guelph and I would finally be free of academia forever, (or so I thought)! Hamilton was still in need of ambulance attendants so I was able to continue working upon my return. It wasn't long though before I had the majority of my debts paid down and felt my feet getting itchy to travel. My near death experiences in France had turned me off rafting a little bit and I needed to find another avenue to explore.

Enter Youth Challenge International (YCI). YCI is a Canadian nonprofit initiative that sends youths, aged 18-25, from Canada, Costa Rica and Australia, to Guyana, South America to perform 3 months of community service work. Prior to leaving, participants must raise $3000 to cover their travel and living expenses while they are down there. I never knew projects like this even existed, but as soon as I heard about it, I knew it was perfect for me.

However, just before learning about YCI, the ambulance service I worked for offered me a full time job and the rafting company I had worked for in the Arctic asked me if I was available to assist them again that summer. The full time ambulance job was just the position my parents always dreamed I would have. A good paying job chalk full of security and stability. The Arctic job was scheduled to run July through August, and YCI would leave in September and return late in November.

I don't think anybody had ever turned down a full time offer from this ambulance service before so my manager was quite surprised when I asked for a 6 month leave of absence instead. I didn't see the problem and was quite surprised when I was told there would be no job at all waiting for me if I attempted to return after a 6 month leave. But that was just a chance I was willing to take.

After another great summer of rafting the Coppermine I received all of my inoculations, packed my bag, and jetted off with 50 other youths to Georgetown, Guyana. Being 24 years old, I was one of the older volunteers on the excursion and with all of my medical training I frequently found myself in a leadership role.

While there I worked on three separate projects. The first was with Street Kids International in Georgetown. This project involved working with the city's growing number of street kids and connecting them with peers from some of the existing youth organizations. There were eight of us on this project and I found myself paired with one of the Costa Rican challengers, Jorge Federico Calderon-Moralez, aka "Feds". Federico didn't speak much English at that time and was generally confused when the instructions and assignments were handed out. To play it safe, he simply shadowed me. I was tall, I must have known what was going on! From my perspective, I didn't like working with a bunch of granola crunching, tree-hugging, do-gooder, hippie-wannabe, teenagers. So Feds and I got along just fine, doing our own thing and discovering our own project to work on.

While visiting the Palms Nursing Home we witnessed 80 year old women on the front lawn washing clothes in the puddles formed by the afternoon rains. During British rule, the Palms had been a majestic building, complete with a full service laundry room. However, the country's infrastructure left with the Brits and over the years the building had fallen to shambles and the laundry room had transformed into a storage room for garbage. Identifying this as a problem that could be solved, Feds and I had a Vision of cleaning out the old laundry facility and breathing new life back into it. The concrete basins were still there and we just needed to reestablish the electricity and the plumbing from the well back to the sinks.

Mike Caldwell

Washing the clothes in a puddle and leaving them to dry on the grass.

Of course, an organization like Youth Challenge International doesn't have the available funds to simply sponsor an initiative like this and Federico and I had to go into the community and request donations for this project. The public response to our project was overwhelming. Although it was an extremely poor country, every hardware "store" in town was willing to contribute whatever they could. Feds and I both had a Vision of our completed project and became more and more excited with each day's success. But we were also working against the clock because a deadline had been set for when we had to leave on our next project. With a week to spare we had compiled all the equipment and tools that would be required. All that was left was the installation. We locked everything up in the tool shed with the plan of returning the following morning to get the job underway.

Upon arrival that morning, we found the lock on the shed broken and every one of our tools and supplies gone. We were devastated. All we could do was call the police and report the crime. But there was good news! The crooks had actually been caught in the act the previous evening and all of the materials were in police custody. What a lucky break! Or so we thought... The stolen material was now "evidence" and couldn't be released until after the trial. And there was no way that was going to happen before Federico and I left on our next project. The only thing we could do was go back to our original contributors, explain the situation and beg them to loan us new material with the promise that their original donations would be returned to them after the trial.

It was certainly an uphill battle but eventually we were able to persuade every donor to help us out again. By this time, we only had a couple of days left and Feds and I had to literally work around the clock to get the laundry room functional before our departure. But we were successful and on our last day in Georgetown we had a ribbon cutting ceremony to open the laundry facility. The room and the clothes drying area turned out exactly the way Federico and I had envisioned it, the only thing not in our original Vision were the smiles and tears on the old ladies faces when they saw what we had done for them.

Federico testing the taps, and the "laundry woman" hanging the clothes

Although it pained us to leave Georgetown, there were still other areas of the country that needed our help. On our next project, Federico and I traveled up the Esequibo River into the heart of the Guyanese rainforest to assist a team of British scientists with a biodiversity study and establish a school and ongoing lessons for the children in the village of Karupakari. The challenge here wasn't in the tasks themselves but rather in basic survival. The only food we had available to us during our five week stay there was: a bag of rice, a bag of flour, a bag of chick peas, a couple tins of tuna, some bread yeast, salt, peanut butter and a few spices. Boiling was the only method of purifying the brown river water we had to drink. This was the only nourishment we had to keep us strong enough for the projects we were expected to complete. I watch television's Survivor™ today and laugh at how easy those individuals have it!

But survive we did and off we traveled to our next project which was in the East Indian village of Mettenmeerzorg. Our task here was to rebuild a school which had similarly fallen to ruin after the departure of British rule. This was a relatively straightforward assignment as we had all the equipment, supplies, food and water that we required. The lessons I learned here were from the locals who assisted us. They were all so kind, considerate, giving and happy. There were very few days when I wasn't invited to somebody's home for dinner. These were very poor, yet proud, people. Dinner was generally comprised of rice, vegetables and maybe some chicken which we would eat with our fingers off a banana leaf. These people didn't have very much, but what they did have they were certainly willing to share and this had a very profound effect on me.

In November I returned to Canada, unemployed but with an entirely new perspective on life. If you are reading this book and are in your late teens or early 20's, or if you have a child or a friend in this age range, I would strongly recommend you research some of the available charitable travel organizations and take part in one of these missions. Actually living in a country that doesn't have all the luxuries and conveniences of the modern world has allowed me to approach each day with a better perspective of what I have and how lucky I am to live in this country.

Luckily, once I returned to Canada, the ambulance service I had previously worked for still had weak management and a strong union, and with little effort I was able to return to work as an ambulance attendant. I was quite content during my first year back home, seeing Canada with the new eyes of understanding I had acquired in South America. But eventually I began to grow restless and knew I wanted more.

The ambulance service I was working for was undertaking a provincial pilot program to study the efficacy of true "paramedic" service. Paramedics have the ability to initiate intravenous lines, administer medications, intubate, perform cricothyrotomies, and aspirate collapsed chests with a needle. Ambulance attendants, like me, could apply band-aids, immobilize potential spinal injuries, and administer oxygen. Hamilton had 13 of these super-medics, and I was assigned as a paramedic partner. Although my main job was to chauffeur and clean up after the medics, I was able to see first hand the procedures they were able to perform.

It was decided. I wanted to be a full-fledged paramedic. The problem was that our base hospital pilot program was not expanding or training new paramedics and there were no rumours that paramedic service would expand to include the rest of the province. There were true paramedics throughout the United States though, and there were schools there to which I could apply. I spoke with my management and the base hospital which oversaw all of our medical acts and was informed that even if I did receive paramedic training in the USA it wouldn't be recognized anywhere in Canada.

But since I had never let a lack of encouragement dissuade me before, I threw hazard to the wind and applied to schools in California, Oregon, Idaho, and Colorado (all

Mike Caldwell

states that possessed great downhill skiing!). And much to my surprise, within a couple of months I was accepted at the Swedish Medical Center six month paramedic program in Denver, Colorado. With only a couple of months to gather funding, I sold whatever I could sell, and worked as many shifts on the ambulance as I could fit into my schedule.

On the evening of June 25th, 1994 I went and saw Pink Floyd perform at the Canadian National Exhibition, and the next day I loaded all of my worldly possessions (mountain bike, road bike, downhill skis, a cooler and a crock pot) into my 1984 Ford Econoline van and headed southwest to Denver. My plan was to find a campground not too far from the school where I would either rent a small trailer, or pitch a large tent to serve as my home during my 6 months of education. I had one full day to search prior to my first day of class but failed to meet with any success.

Our first class was on a Friday morning and served to simply introduce us to the building, meet our instructors and collect our books. We were out of there by 11am and I had the remainder of the day and the entire weekend to explore Colorado. My first mission was to check out Boulder, the home of Mork and Mindy! I was cruising along the I-25 when all of sudden my van started screaming and grinding and veered onto the shoulder of the highway. This wasn't good. Something was very broken! Luckily I was a member of the automobile club and a tow truck hauled my broken down van to the nearest garage.

I'm not a mechanic and I can't completely remember what went wrong. I know there were brakes, and shoes, tie rods, and stabilizers involved and I know the enormous repair bill wasn't something I had budgeted for! This was definitely not the way I had envisioned starting my Colorado education. But with a huge chunk of my savings now gone, I had to look for areas to cut my expenses. I needed to eat, and I would definitely need gas for the van and supplies for school. So the only way to save some money was to live "on the streets" and not establish a permanent residence. My van was equipped with a bed, cupboards, a closet, a cooler, and camp cooking supplies. And luckily I had membership at a fitness club in Hamilton that was a part of a larger family of clubs in the USA. So my Hamilton membership (which I had actually cancelled before I left) would work at the gym in Denver. So there I had a place to pass the time, exercise, and most importantly SHOWER!

It wasn't long before I had a great system in place. One of my classmates had an apartment close to the hospital and he allowed me to come over every Sunday night and set up my crock pot. He would simply turn it on before he left for class on Monday morning, and that would be the meal he and I would eat on Monday night. There was a Safeway grocery store right across the street from the hospital and this was where I would park my van and "store" most of my food. The school had a small freezer where I could make ice for my cooler, a bathroom that I could access first thing in the morning and a sink where I could wash my dishes. I would basically eat crock pot leftovers for most of the week and supplement that with the odd take-out meal or invitation from a classmate who took pity on me.

It really wasn't a bad system either. I had no commute to class, no rent to pay, and no distractions like television to keep me away from my studies. During my lessons we had a psychologist come it to speak to us about the stress involved with paramedic work and we were all asked to share a stressful experience in our lives. When it came around to me I said, "I'm in the country illegally (I had failed to get my student visa in time), I am homeless, near penniless, and living in my van in a grocery store parking lot, I have just been diagnosed with Tuberculosis (yeah, I tested positive for TB while in Denver) and I have no potential opportunities for employment upon graduation". Keep in mind the title of this book: V.E.A.R. –Vision, Energy, Attitude, and Resolve. I definitely had to have all four of these bullets firing on all cylinders if I was going to survive a punishing paramedic program while living in the Safeway parking lot and taking my Tuberculosis meds.

But not only did I survive the program but I graduated at the top of my class. Near the end of my program I had also started dating a classmate and at the time of graduation we had both grown rather fond of one another. Here was yet another challenge; Carolyn and I both had feelings for one another but we had only been dating a short time. The United States government gave us 2 choices: 1) I return to Canada and never see Carolyn again, or 2) we get married. This was a tough decision because had there been no immigration laws pressuring us, we would have continued a normal dating relationship and let our story unfold naturally. But given these external governmental pressures, the only way we could stay together and learn if we were right for one another was to get married!

Unfortunately a "shotgun wedding" is never a good idea and this "marriage" was a total disaster. In the weeks leading up to our nuptials, both Carolyn and I realized that marriage probably wasn't the best choice for the two of us. But the church and caterer were already reserved, the rings and flowers ordered and it foolishly just seemed easier to go ahead and get married. In this book you're going to read about "failing your way to success". This is a perfect example of how I was able to learn the lessons from one failure and apply them to what I consider to be a near-perfect relationship now.

During my five year stay in Colorado and two year marriage, I was fortunate enough to live some amazing experiences and pick up my Master's Degree. I was hired on by a fire department not only as a firefighter but as the company's medical officer. I was encouraged to expand a basic life support service to an advanced life support service and increase the level of service provided by the volunteers. In another job, I was also given the opportunity to work alone in a hospital emergency department. Normally, this is the job of ER nurses, but due to a lack of available nurses and hospital funding, the ER was staffed by paramedics. During the evenings and weekends, there wasn't even a doctor on the hospital grounds – he would be on-call from home. So regardless of what injury or illness came in, I was completely on my own to deal with it until a physician or physician's assistant arrived. I remember one episode when the physician never arrived at all! We called him at the clinic, and we called his house, we paged his pager, and paged him overhead within the hospital. But he was in the doctor's lounge running on the treadmill with his Walkman on. He never heard any of the pages and I was alone and responsible for ordering all the necessary tests and prescribing treatment. What a rush! (And yes, the patient did very well by the way.)

But after five years in Colorado, I finally decided it was time to return to the country I loved, Canada. I still had the same van, but on my return trip home I had to purchase a trailer and build a big box on the roof to transport my motorcycle and all of my US acquisitions. Once again, I was starting with next to nothing. I had my van, my motorcycle, a bread maker, a 19" colour television, two Border Collies, and $37 in the bank. I had nowhere to go but up! Fortunately the unexpected had occurred while I was away and paramedics and paramedic training had been introduced province wide. I initially had to jump through a few hoops, but again using V.E.A.R. I was able to secure reciprocity through Sunnybrook Hospital and be certified as an advanced care flight paramedic in Ontario.

My goal was to find employment in Ottawa. I had fallen in love with this region during my time as a raft guide and desperately hoped I would be able to make this my home. Unfortunately for me, Ottawa is strongly bilingual and with my lack of competency in the French language I was not eligible for many of the jobs there. I was eventually able to create a position for myself doing a diabetic "treat and release" research study through Sunnybrook Hospital and was commuting back and forth to Toronto from Hamilton. I've never been a fan of big cities and commuting certainly wasn't for me either. I expanded my job search and interviewed for a paramedic position in Kingston.

On the day that I was expecting to hear the results from Kingston, the telephone rang and it was a representative from Canadian Helicopters. My name had been passed along to them from Sunnybrook Hospital and they wanted to know if I'd be willing to work as the supervisor for the newly established Preferred Provider Air Ambulance Program in Ottawa! After confirming this was not a hoax I agreed to not only hire and supervise the Ottawa helicopter paramedics, but spearhead initiating the entire program province wide.

This was not only an amazing opportunity, but the dream of every paramedic in the country. I was not only going to be working on a helicopter, but I would have all the latest in medical technology and the backing of the most progressive base hospital in Canada. Before I knew it, I had purchased a home near the airport, a cottage in the Gatineau Hills, a new car and new mountain bike. Initially I thought life couldn't get any better, but then the demands of being a supervisor and the politics of the industry began to get to me.

Flying past Toronto's CN Tower and Skydome on our way to a transfer from Sick Kid's Hospital.

As I grew older, responding to calls in the middle of the night or on the frigid, winter, windswept highways began to take its toll on me. I knew I would eventually need a change of career, one with less stress and normal business hours. So I started Corporate Synergy as a part time gig. My plan was to provide corporate team building and leadership development training to Ottawa's highly profitable high tech sector. Bit by bit I developed my plan, and expanded on my business ideas. I even started to attract the odd client.

Part of my business was getting people to expand their comfort zones by challenging themselves in high rope obstacles. Rappelling was one of the tools I would use toward this end. One day, while out on my own establishing a new rappel route, I was "lucky" enough to lose my footing and plummet 32 feet to the rocky ground below. After being awoken by my dog Fred, I realized I had just taken a very serious fall. I knew my arm and leg were broken, but I was more concerned about bleeding to death from potential internal hemorrhaging. Although disoriented and in considerable pain, I had no choice but to limp out a half kilometer back to my cabin, my girlfriend, Monique, and her sister.

Luckily Monique's sister is a nurse and after a quick assessment they drove me to the nearest telephone where an ambulance could be called for my one hour transport to the hospital. Upon exam there, it was learned that I had broken my left arm, my left leg, and my lower back. Surgery was required for my arm, but the other two fractures were simple and non life-threatening. But I certainly wouldn't be working as a paramedic for quite some time!

And this is why I refer to that fall as "lucky". This downtime gave me the opportunity to not only re-assesses what I wanted to do with my life, but it also gave me the opportunity to search the internet for a new place to do it. This is the origin of my work in the field of team building and leadership development and the purchase of "the Ark".

Let the story begin...

Introduction

Have you ever had a dream that you felt was out of reach? Maybe you felt you didn't have enough money, or the right education. Maybe you aren't tall enough or fit enough. Maybe dreams like that are for other people, but certainly not for somebody like you!

Allow me to describe somebody for you and you can try and guess who she is. This woman was born into poverty in 1954. Her mother was an 18 year old girl who knew she was in no position to raise a child. So she moved to Milwaukee to find work while she left her baby to live with her grandmother in rural poverty in Mississippi. At age 6, her grandmother became ill and she rejoined her mother and half sister in a Milwaukee boarding house. At age 9 her uncle, cousin and a family "friend" began molesting her. At age 14, she became pregnant herself and gave birth to a child two months premature. The baby, a boy, died two weeks following its birth.

This girl certainly had no money, no connections, and minimal family support. With a start in life such as this, who would blame her if she never succeeded at anything? Fortunately, this woman believed in herself and fought all of her life until she came to the point where she has recently been called "the most influential woman on the planet". Yes, this is the story of Oprah Winfrey.

Finding excuses is always easy. Staying focused through both the good times and the bad requires strength. Do I think it was 14 year old Oprah's intention to be the wealthiest, most influential woman on the planet one day? No, probably not. But I do think every day she awoke with a dream of making a better life for herself. Oprah Winfrey didn't become "Oprah" over night. It was a step by step and goal by goal process, with each goal being bigger and grander than the last. And since Oprah never set any limitations on herself, she just never stopped reaching for the stars.

This is where you should stand with your goals. I think you need to dream big, but stay grounded with smaller, intermediate steps along the way. Currently I'm 39 years old and I feel I have accomplished quite a bit in life. I've traveled Canada, the United States, Europe, the Arctic, and Central and South America. I'm very happily married and presently share a home with two high Energy, loyal and loving border collies. I'm very healthy and fit enough to run a complete 26.2 mile marathon. We now own a 6,000 square foot, off-the-grid, solar home on 164 acres of prime Gatineau Hills real estate, two newer cars, and tons of toys for playing in the outdoors. We usually vacation twice a year and every second winter we spend a couple of weeks on the beaches of Costa Rica.

Although I am quite proud of these accomplishments, most of these things are only possessions. What I am most proud of is that I have always lived my life on my terms. I've traveled extensively, made many friends, and except for that one summer in the box factory, I have never worked a day in my life at a job I didn't want to be doing. I've been a raft guide, an ambulance attendant, a firefighter, an emergency room technician, a community developer, a substitute high school teacher and a helicopter paramedic. These are all fun and exciting jobs, and some of them didn't pay all that badly either! I am now married to the woman of my dreams, working on the career of my dreams, and living in the location of my dreams.

So how did I do it?

V.E.A.R.

Vision, Energy, Attitude, Resolve.

Rinse and repeat.

In each step of my life I saw exactly what I wanted before I got there. I could not only see it, but I heard it, smelled it, tasted it, and felt it. It was real in my mind, long before it was real in the world. This is not to say I found a magic lamp and a genie provided me with 3 wishes. Why was I hired as the medical officer at the Fire Department? Why did a get to work as a paramedic flying around in a multi-million dollar helicopter? Well, primarily because I was a trained paramedic, but the only reason that happened was because I was willing to live in a van in a Safeway parking lot to make it happen.

Having a Vision was just the first step. Energy was required from there. It's cold in Denver in December, and some mornings it took all the Energy I could muster to get out from underneath those covers and put on those cold, stiff clothes. One morning I couldn't brush my teeth because my toothpaste was frozen! Yes, Energy was definitely a factor. I had to gather that Energy from deep within myself to keep going and when that wasn't enough I borrowed Energy from my friends, family, classmates and coworkers.

Equally important though is Attitude. Staying positive is absolutely imperative. Like Mark Twain said,

> "If you think you can, or think you can't, you're probably right" – Mark Twain

I never allowed myself to believe that what I wanted to do wasn't possible. I knew I couldn't speak French when I left for France but that wasn't going to stop me from guiding rafts over there. If I needed to learn a new language, then that is simply what I would do. I've never done anything that hasn't been done by somebody else before and my motto is: "if it can be done, it can be done by me".

And last, but certainly not least, comes Resolve. Some people have argued that this is the most important trait in realizing your goals. I still believe that it is equally weighted with Vision, Energy and Attitude. In those first pages of Background information I mentioned a few of the trials and tribulations I faced along my journey. But only a few. For every success I have ever achieved there are five stories of the universe working against me. When Federico and I arrived at the Palms Nursing Home to find all of our supplies gone, we thought we were done. How could we replace in a day what it took us a week to procure? But Federico had dealt with setbacks before in Costa Rica and if we still had three days left in which to fight, he was prepared to go down swinging. Giving up for him wasn't an option. And so we stuck with it, and in the 11th hour, success was ours.

Have you ever been watching television and one of those weight loss commercials comes on? They'll show you the story of half a dozen individuals who all weighed in excess of 300 pounds, and then after six weeks of simply drinking two milkshakes a day they are all qualifying to run the Boston Marathon. But if you look at the small print at the bottom of the screen you see a super tiny disclaimer that states "results are not typical".

Well I want you to look at the bottom of this page right now. What do you see in the fine print down there? The book title and page number, that's it. There are no disclaimers to V.E.A.R. It worked for me and it will work for you. My results ARE typical. If you want to succeed, you simply have to lose the excuses and make it happen. There are no secrets here and there are no shortcuts. It's simply a matter of knowing what you want and how bad you really want it.

I've always wanted a red '65 Ford Mustang convertible, but I'll never have one. Why? Because I don't want it badly enough. I'm not willing to sacrifice the minivan I use to transport my bikes and canoes and haul my lumber and friends around. I definitely want a '65 Mustang, but I'm just not prepared to sacrifice or pay the price required to get one.

Here's a little trick to learn how important any dream, goal or Vision is to you. All you need is a stopwatch and some quality alone time! Simply sit or lie down someplace quiet. Start the stopwatch and begin to create your Vision in your mind. Think about and develop that Vision for as long as you can. As soon as you realize that you changed your focus away from that Vision, click the stopwatch again.

How long were you able to concentrate for? If it's any less than 15 minutes, you should probably try again at another time. But if you're still not able to hold and develop that one thought, you may want to reassess your current goal. Where did your thoughts travel to? Perhaps that will give you a clue to what is truly important to you.

If I were to visualize that red Ford Mustang, I'm sure I could see it plain as day sitting in my driveway. I can imagine opening the door, sitting down and firing up the engine. I could picture myself pulling out of the driveway and cruising down the highway. My Vision ends there. I have no idea what I would do next. I'd probably take the car to some nice trails for hiking or mountain biking, or perhaps I'd find a way to transport my canoe with it and go on a trip that way. Obviously, the car is not a priority!

Mike Caldwell

I also want this book to sell 10,000 copies. THAT will happen. How am I going to make that happen? To be honest, as I write this I can't really say right now. But if in the future I'm asked to go on the road and tour the bookstores to help promote it, I will. I am prepared to make that sacrifice and whatever other sacrifice is necessary to make this book a success.

To continue with this example, I can see the new cover of my book on store shelves. At the top of the jacket it says "3rd Edition, Over 10,000 Copies Sold". I can hear the store owner when he calls asking if I'd be willing to come in and sign some books. I can feel the Energy in the room when I talk to the people who enjoyed the book.

I am going to put as much Energy into this thing as required. I know people are going to tell me they've read this book before. "It's the same as the other success books out there". But my Attitude is unwavering. I'll acknowledge that perception but I know this book is different. I didn't beat cancer and I didn't go from living on the streets to the wealthiest person on the planet. I simply wanted to live a life whereby I am happy and excited every day. I wanted to live in a modest house in the woods with the woman of my dreams and I made those things happen. These are goals, dreams, and aspirations each one of us shares and that is why this book is different. I know I'm going to have a tough time convincing most people of that. But showing Resolve, I will not give up and I will continue to spread the word until I am heard.

What is your goal?

What do you want out of life?

What would you have to accomplish to consider yourself successful?

I'm telling you right here and right now, that regardless of what your answers are to those questions, you can make it happen. It's simply a matter of V.E.A.R.

Part 1

Vision

Clarity of Vision

"If one advances confidently in the direction of their dreams, and endeavours to lead a life which they have imagined, they will meet with success unexpected in common hours." - Thoreau

Every goal that you ever want to realize must be created twice; first in your mind and then in the world. The more real you can make the image in your head, the better the likelihood of your success. When you wish to conjure a dream in your mind, don't just think of the word over and over again. Create a tangible 3 dimensional image in your mind's eye and then further animate that image with sounds, thoughts, smells and feelings.

> You have to See it, Hear it, Smell it and Feel it BEFORE you can Be it.

Try this exercise. Let's assume you are tired of sleeping restlessly at night and you would like a new bed. Take a break from this page and for the next few seconds think to yourself "I want a new bed. I want a new bed. I want a new bed."

Did you do it? I hope so. Now regardless of whether you wanted a new bed this morning or not, do you want a new bed now?

Probably not.

Now try this exercise. Imagine a long hard day either at work, or with the kids, or exercising, or whatever. You are physically and mentally drained and you want nothing more than to lie down and rest. All your responsibilities for the day are behind you and you step into the bathroom for a nice hot shower or bubble bath (this is your Vision so it's up to you!). You towel off afterward, slip into a nice plush robe and walk back to the bedroom. When you enter you see your new bed in front of you. There are soft, fluffy pillows at the headboard and a big lush duvet covering the bed. You drop your robe and slip under the covers. The sheets are freshly washed, crisp and provide a soothing scent. You dissolve into the Pillowtop mattress as the bed and down pillows envelop you. As you relax further into the bed, you feel all of your stresses melt away. You close your eyes and feel warm, relaxed, and safe. As you drift to sleep, you dream of warm ocean breezes and carefree frivolities. The next morning you awake to the smell of fresh baked muffins and hot coffee. That special someone has prepared breakfast in bed before slipping in beside you. You roll over and snuggle into that person, realizing that eventually you'll have to depart from this nest, but in the meantime you're going to savor every moment.

Okay, how about now? Do you want a new bed now???

It's all about advertising in your mind. You have to sell yourself on your idea and convince yourself that this is something you really want. If you tell yourself you want a new bed and picture the mattress wrapped in plastic leaning up against the wall, how badly are you going to work for that mattress? But if you paint a picture like I have a couple of paragraphs earlier your mind is much more likely to strive towards that goal. And just like a television commercial, the more this Vision is played, the more the advertisement works itself into your very core.

> Your subconscious doesn't know the difference between what is real and imagined.

Have you ever awoken in the middle of the night after having a nightmare? Your heart is racing, your breathing is heavy, and your body is covered in sweat. Your mind had created an intense and frightening storyline, and your subconscious was not aware that the nightmare wasn't real. Your subconscious doesn't know the difference between fantasy and reality. It only looks to and responds to that which is happening in your mind.

If you link that new bed to feelings of happiness and pleasure, your subconscious is going to respond in kind, releasing endorphins into the bloodstream, and creating a positive loop. These endorphins are a drug just like heroin or cocaine, and your body will become addicted to them. If your subconscious starts to link that new bed to that endorphin high, what do you think your subconscious will do to make that bed a reality? Just like a junkie looking for his next fix, your subconscious will do whatever it needs to do to succeed.

If you can work with your subconscious towards a goal, rather than against it, your odds of success have just increased exponentially. I say this because just as beneficial as your subconscious can be, it can also be your biggest enemy. Successful people live in the present and drive forward, strongly targeted on the future. Unsuccessful people tend to live in the past and relive their failures or disappointments over and over again in their minds.

Let's assume you are currently single but looking for a new relationship. Do you spend most of your time thinking about the qualities of your new significant other and how you will feel in that relationship? Or, do frequently think about your past three relationships and how unhappy those made you, especially when they ended. If you continue to associate negative emotions with your relationships, what is that teaching your subconscious? It is learning that relationships equal pain and sadness. Your subconscious is hardwired to avoid negative feelings. It has been said that there are really only two motivators in life: the pursuit of pleasure and the avoidance of pain. Have you ever heard anybody say that it's like subconsciously you want to fail? If past experiences have linked your current goal to negative emotions, then it may be true that subconsciously you do want to fail!

> Two Motivators in Life: The pursuit of happiness and the avoidance of pain.

This is why positive imagery is so important. You need to minimize any negative influence your current goal might create. Perhaps you have applied for that promotion three times already, but each time they have given the job to somebody else. Well, perhaps now it is your turn. Did you know Michael Jordan was cut from his high school basketball team? Or did you know that Dr. Seuss had his first book rejected by 23 publishers? My motto is, "if it can be done, it can be done by me". If that promotion truly is a goal, then continue to use V.E.A.R. and eventually you will succeed.

> If it can be done, it can be done by me

<u>Vision and Corporate Synergy</u>

Last year at around this time I submitted a proposal to provide a day of team building to 200 government employees. At the time, I thought it was an excellent proposal and was actually surprised when I was not successful with my bid. But upon receiving my "letter of regret", I contacted the contracting authority and asked why my services were not chosen. I learned that my proposal was very similar to the event the client had experienced the previous year, and that this year they were looking for something a little different.

So this spring I sent a letter to that contracting authority again, reminding her that I was still available for team building events and advising her that I had expanded upon my programming options. Three weeks ago I was contacted by a new contracting authority, now representing the same client and was asked to submit another proposal for this year's event. Prior to doing so, I contacted this year's contract authority and asked more specific questions related to this year's goals and objectives. This year I knew exactly what the client was looking for and specifically how to word my proposal. Three days ago I was hired to lead this year's session.

> Don't be afraid to learn from your mistakes.

In applying for the contract this year I had no worry or apprehension at all. Yes, my proposal was rejected last summer, but it was nothing personal. My competition had simply presented a program that was more in line with the client's goals and objectives. Last summer I learned that if I wanted to be successful in this business I needed to add more dimensions to my programming. Initially my business was solely focused on experiential education (EE) and I still believe that this is the best medium for adult education. However, there are those clients who would rather not explore EE and there are venues in which it is simply not appropriate. Thus, for the past year I have worked on organization development, team building, and leadership development seminars and my presentation skills. I have also added motivational and keynote speaking to my repertoire, and now I'm writing a book!

In recent years I have had a Vision for my success. My Vision is not a static picture; rather it is an ongoing scene that unfolds within my mind. I picture myself at my high ropes course and my clients are working their way through a specifically difficult challenge. The sun is shining, the leaves are green, the air is fresh, and through the forest I can hear the screams of laughter from another group working their way through their obstacles. From this picture, the image flashes to the lunch break; people are sitting together at the tables outside laughing and sharing stories of their morning's adventures. I notice the manager sitting at one of the tables and it is obvious that she is fitting right in and is completely accepted by the people who work for her. Once more the scene flashes to the afternoon debriefing session and ideas and workplace solutions are flowing at a furious rate. Real progress is being made and you can tell people are expecting positive change back at the office.

In my mind, this is the best program ever! I spent so much time developing it, and tweaking every parameter, yet from time to time my proposal is not accepted. How can this be? Why would a company not want to be involved in a program like this? There have been times when I have been desperate for money, the phone rings, and it's a potential client requesting a proposal. I really need this job and give my absolute best effort in customizing the project and giving the best value I can offer. I get so excited because this job will save me (temporarily) from my financial woes. But then a week or two later, I receive the "letter of regret". I didn't get the job and now my financial concerns are even worse than before.

There is the potential for some very strong negative reinforcement to be established here. I created a tremendous program, found a potential client, but was refused and came out empty handed. What if this happens again? And again the time after that? I felt terrible the first time and I know I'll just feel even worse with each subsequent incident. This has the potential to really worry me. So what is the Vision I am creating now?

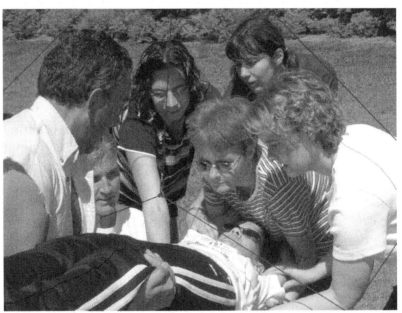

Here's a team strongly focused on not touching any of the strands of the spider's web as they pass a coworker through.

It is one of failure and disappointment. I am actually now creating a roadmap to failure. See how easy this is to do. Alternatively, I can use that initial "failure" as a learning and motivational tool. There is still nothing wrong with my initial Vision, it is still exactly what some of my potential clients are looking for. In this most recent example, the client loved my concept but it was just not something they were looking for at this time. Here is an opportunity for a new, but parallel, Vision.

This is me doing my "V.E.A.R." presentation for employees at Statistics Canada, January, 2008.

In my new Vision I am standing at the front of a large conference room, I am wearing a suit jacket and a wireless microphone headset. Behind me there is a large PowerPoint presentation being projected and in front there are 300 people focused entirely on me and hanging on my every word. I'm giving a presentation on leadership development, I make a joke and on cue, everybody laughs. The scene then flashes to my closing remarks and the conclusion of the conference. Instead of leaving, a number of individuals work their way to the front either to thank me for my talk or to discuss some of my concepts further. This is a completely different venue, but my success is just as great here.

Now I have another Vision to strive for and work towards. I'm not saying all I have to do is think it and it will become real. I don't have a magic genie remember and this book is entitled V.E.A.R. This is only the "V", the first step. But without the "V" you have nowhere to focus your "E", "A", or "R".

Share Your Vision

This next piece of advice should not be considered a hard-fast rule, rather a suggestion to be considered based on the application. For some Visions and for a couple of reasons, I believe it is important to tell others of your dreams, goals or intentions. There are some goals in which having a support network is absolutely critical. Let's return to that example in which you are striving toward a promotion at work but have been denied in your last three attempts. In a situation like this it is not difficult to begin to lose faith in yourself. From your perspective you have done everything and worked yourself as hard as you possibly could. But still that promotion has been denied you. Maybe you just aren't good enough...

This is where sharing your Vision with someone who has faith in you is so important. This person may be your spouse, a boyfriend, a girlfriend, a friend, a coworker or a family member. What is important here is that this person believes in you and can see your situation from a more objective perspective. The role of this individual is to ensure you don't lose sight of your Vision. This person needs to refresh that Vision in your mind for you every day. They need to remind you why you chose that goal to begin with and what the rewards are going to be.

This person may even be able to give you some insight on where you are going wrong or why you haven't yet been successful. Perhaps you believe you are doing everything you can to earn that promotion; you are arriving at work earlier, leaving work later, and landing more accounts than anybody else in your office. But perhaps you don't have the same academic accomplishments as the people who have been promoted ahead of you, or perhaps you only speak one language and they all have spoken two. Of course you don't see why any of this should matter because you have proven that you can produce better results despite these "shortcomings". This is another area in which your support person plays their role. Somebody needs to sit you down and tell you that although you are smart, motivated, and highly productive, management regulations are what they are and if you want to advance you'll need to start taking some part time classes or learn that second language. Once again, V.E.A.R. isn't easy, but if you have Vision and focus your Energy in the right direction, success will be yours. There are just times when you need a friend to reinforce that Vision and help you focus that Energy.

You don't need to go it alone, external support could be just the boost you need to put you over the top.

In this example it is obvious that your support will share and believe in your dream with you. But sharing the dream is not absolutely necessary; all that is important is that your supporter believes in you. I have a friend who just ran 7,000km across the Sahara Desert from coast to coast, running two marathons a day, day after day without a single day's rest, for 111 days straight. To be honest, I never believed this feat was humanly possible and I thought it to be an unrealistic goal. But although I didn't believe the goal was possible I did believe in my friend and did everything I could do to stay positive and support him any way I could.

That is an example of a goal that is literally bigger than life. But not every goal that requires support needs to be so grandiose. In fact yesterday I spoke to a friend with whom I haven't been in contact for quite some time. For his birthday this past summer, his wife collected donations from all of his friends and family in order to purchase a combined gift of a flight to Germany. He is going alone and his wife is sending him so that he may accomplish two of his life goals: 1) to witness the Tour de France cycling race, and 2) to drive a Porsche at high speeds down the German Autobahn!

Every year millions of spectators line the roads of France to witness the toughest endurance event on the planet. So wanting to be a part of that is not all that crazy, but driving a Porsche on the Autobahn???? For many of us, that dream may seem foolish, reckless, and frivolous, but for my friend this is a dream he has long envisioned. Had he not shared this dream with his wife, in all likelihood it would never have been realized. His wife may not share this dream, but she believes in her husband.

Brad's photos from the Tour de France and driving the Autobahn.

Another reason to share your goals is not for support, but rather for accountability. For years I had dreamed of competing in an Ironman triathlon (2.4 mile swim, 112 mile bike, 26.2 mile run). But year after year I found some excuse not to register or compete. Completing an Ironman race takes a long term commitment to training and proper nutrition, and I have never been overly enthusiastic on either of these disciplines. But unlike that red Ford Mustang, completing an Ironman event was something important for me to include in my life's accomplishments.

Here in Ottawa, we have a weekday morning, triathlon based, community-supported newsletter called TriRudy.com. There are currently 5000 members and each day every member has the opportunity to include a post within the next morning's newsletter. Generally people contribute advice on training, nutrition, equipment, etc. or they may provide race reports, or advertise some sports related equipment in the Classified section. Of course in any community-based forum there is the odd posting on a more personal level. I frequently post race reports on this site and initiate debates on wetsuit use and training principles. So I have established myself as one of the better known site contributors and have a contingent of people who either like to support or debate me. Anyhow, the point of this story is that early in 2005 I announced to the 4,000+ members that after competing in a multitude of short distance triathlons, I would be attempting an Iron Distance race later that summer and I would be competing in it without wearing a wetsuit!

By boldly announcing this to the masses I now had some accountability. I had established a reputation within the TriRudy community and if I failed to follow through with my announcement all credibility would be lost. Not only did I make this announcement "public" on TriRudy, along the way I also made a prediction that I would beat a strong, well known, local racer at another shorter event earlier in the summer. In reality, it would be unlikely that I could beat this individual, but week after week I would post comments on the website and close with the prediction that "Giles is Going Down!"

Thus I had increased motivation during my training sessions. Not only did I know I had to get the miles in or risk not having the confidence to even make it to the Ironman starting line. But I also had to get in some quality miles if I had any chance at all of beating Giles, or at least not embarrassing myself in the process.

So I had to create Visions for both of these events. I'm going to talk about my Ironman Vision in the pages to come, but for my short distance triathlon showdown with Giles I had the entire event hardwired in my head by the time race day arrived. I'm a strong swimmer and Giles is fast on the run. In most triathlons, the run section is weighted much heavier than the swim portion and a strong runner will beat a strong swimmer in the overall standings every time. But in this event, the swim was longer and the run was shorter than usual. So although Giles did have an advantage, it wasn't as pronounced as it might have been in any other race. On the bike we were equally matched, although being lighter than me he would have the advantage on this extremely hilly course.

To even the field even more, Giles agreed to race me without the benefit provided by the buoyancy of a wetsuit. So in my Vision I could see Giles and I standing on the beach in our bathing suits in a sea of wetsuit clad participants. I would be standing front and center and prepared to sprint into the water as soon as the gun sounded. With my long legs I would be able to run into the lake further than many of my competitors and sprint into an early lead. With Giles being shorter and less confident in the swim he would be trapped back in the masses fighting to possess his own little space within the lake. Conversely, I would be out in front in the lead pack in a streamlined and drafting position moving gracefully unhindered through the water. My arm strokes would be long and strong, I would be kicking rhythmically and efficiently, and I would attain maximum glide and minimum resistance from the water. My breathing would be relaxed, regular and controlled and I would exit the water with the majority of the pack still far behind me.

Here I am starting my watch on my way into the water. Why am I the only guy NOT wearing a wetsuit?

I had also gone through the sequence of the transition from the swim to the bike over and over again in my mind. I would jog briskly across the sand to my bike, all the while attempting to keep my breathing under control. I would step into the pan of clean water to rinse the sand from my feet before sitting down on my folded towel to put on my shoes. To save time I had decided to race without socks and my shoes would slide on effortlessly. I would then stand up and clasp my race bib belt around my waist. In the same motion I would remove my sunglasses from my upturned helmet and place them on before donning my lid. I'd grab my bike from the rack and jog out through the exit and onto the road.

Without skipping a beat, I'd mount my bike and find the gear that I could pedal at 90rpm. I knew I needed to stay focused during this ride and maximize each pedal stroke. I would have no idea how large my lead was over Giles, but I knew every second would count as we began the run. So I would focus on staying in the zone, spinning as hard as I could on the uphills, and staying as aerodynamic as possible on the downhills. Near the end of the bike I would concentrate on dropping my heels just a little more to stretch my hamstrings and prepare for the run.

The run I had envisioned much the same as the bike. I couldn't worry about where Giles was, I just had to focus on what my body was capable of doing and maximizing that. I envisioned running with my head high, arms swinging rhythmically front and back and a shortened but relaxed stride with a high turnover count. In my Vision, I could picture the finish line ahead, but I could also see Giles not far behind. I knew I would have to dig deep over that last few hundred meters and give it everything I had. In my mind I could hear Giles's footsteps and even his breathing as we both approached the line, but I used this stress to pump up my adrenaline, push all that much harder and edge out Giles by a nose as we crossed the line together.

It was this Vision that I would use time and again during my training. I knew this was going to be a tough race and if I was going to be able to succeed in the manner I saw it within my mind, I was going to have to pay my dues beforehand.

"But what actually happened race day?" you ask. Well on the morning of the race we awoke to thunderstorms. The roads were all soaking wet with large puddles all over the place. Given the extreme hills on the bike course, for safety concerns, the bike leg of the event had to be cancelled and the run extended by nearly 50%. So my odds of actually defeating Giles had decreased significantly! But my mental preparation had not gone to waste. My swim had unfolded just as I had imagined it, and my run too went extremely well. Giles swimming had improved considerably the previous winter but even he was surprised when it took him nearly 6km to catch me. In the end, I beat Giles by 2 minutes out of the water and he beat me by 4 minutes on the run, resulting in my 2 minute defeat.

This exercise wasn't in vain though as training to beat Giles in this race gave me a higher level of fitness on the day of Ironman. And finishing within 2 minutes of such an accomplished racer did not hurt my credibility despite the loss. Thus in this instance sharing this Vision with the TriRudy masses provided me with the accountability I required to stay focused and not disappoint those who believed in and supported me.

> By making your Vision public, you increase your accountability and your motivation to succeed.

However, at the same time there was another challenge I had set for myself but didn't share with anybody else. Along with the TriRudy community, the founder had also created a much coveted "Rudy Award". This award is presented to any individual who completes the following events in one calendar year: the Winterlude Tri (a winter triathlon that incorporates an 8km skate on the Rideau Canal, followed by a 4.5km cross country ski and a 5km run), the Keskinada 54km Ski Loppet, the Rideau Lakes Cycle Tour (a 180km bike tour – each way – from Ottawa to Kingston and back), a 26.2 mile running marathon, and an Ironman triathlon.

Ironman had long been a dream of mine and something important for me to accomplish. By sharing this dream with the masses I had the pressures of accountability, but the Rudy Award was something that would be fun for me to try but not something to which I was committed. Nobody ever expected somebody like me would complete the Rudy Award (I didn't own any cross country skis and I hated to run!), so it would be fun to surprise them if, at the end of the year, I was successful. But if I failed to complete all the events, it would be no big deal to me and not something others would consider me a failure for not completing.

Be Selective When Sharing

Before you make your goals public or before you even simply confide in that one friend, be sure it is something you are serious about. Supporting a friend can take a lot of Energy. This is Energy most of us don't mind expending if we feel it is being put to good use, but it can be very frustrating if we feel it is being wasted. Let's say I tell my friend I would really love a red 1965 Ford Mustang. He doesn't say anything to me but he knows his uncle has this very car being stored in a garage and doesn't drive it anymore. So he goes to uncle and asks if he would be willing to sell the vehicle. Initially, his uncle says "no", but through persistent urging he convinces his uncle that if he sells the car he could take that around the world vacation he has always dreamed of. The car is easily worth $12,000, but my friend convinces him to sell it to me for $7,000 because it's guaranteed I'll take good care of it.

My friend just went to great lengths to make my dream a reality for me. But what happens when he comes to me and tells me that he has a mint condition, cherry red, 1965 Ford Mustang available to me for only $7,000 and I say "thanks, but no thanks". It sounds like a great deal but I had already planned on building a new deck on my house this summer and that will eat most of my savings.

Just how important was my red Mustang goal to me? When will I ever have another opportunity like that? If I really wanted that car, I would make it happen. Either I would postpone building that deck or I would get a loan so that I could own that car. But obviously, if I'm not willing to make even the slightest sacrifice for this vehicle, it is a "dream" that will probably never be realized.

As for my friend, how is he going to feel when he tells his uncle he'll have to postpone that vacation he got him so excited about. His uncle even agrees to drop the price to $6,000 but my friend knows I still won't go for it. Obviously this car isn't very high on my list of priorities. So what's going to happen next time I go to my friend for help? "Hey buddy, I just wrote this great book I'm calling V.E.A.R., my goal is to sell 10,000 copies. Do you know anybody who might want to buy one?"

I'm sure his response will be, "let me think about it and I'll get back to you."

I'll never see that friend again! Having people for support and accountability can be critical to your success in achieving your Vision, but use these resources wisely. The people don't have to believe in your goal, but they do need to believe in you. If you lose that, you are on your own and left with nothing.

> Your support network is a valuable resource, use it wisely.

Fail Your Way To Success

Failure is an excellent opportunity for growth. I personally don't truly learn how to do something right until I have done it wrong at least once. Think about it for a second, how many times are you rewarded for doing something right? Probably not that often. So what is there to draw attention to that act? Nothing. But what happens when you do something wrong? I'm sure the majority of the time there are repercussions that you are unlikely to forget!

Mike Caldwell

Let's say nobody ever told you not to play with fire. What do you think is going to happen the first time you play with fire? Sure, you're going to get burned. And what follows from that? Well firstly, you'll never play with fire again and secondly you'll probably share this information with your friends and loved ones. This will result in them never having to get burned themselves. But what if you went through life never coming into contact with fire? You're doing the "right thing" by not playing with it, but at the same time you are unable to maximize your potential because you don't have the knowledge to share and protect others.

In building the Ark, I had more than my fair share of failures. Keep in mind that prior to purchasing this property, I had no experience with any construction or carpentry related endeavours. In fact, looking back it's frightening to imagine just how naïve and ignorant I was.

The first time I ever hung drywall I simply lined the first sheet up with the outside wall, and where that sheet ended, it ended. In that case, that first sheet didn't end lined up with a stud. Rather, it just hung out there in open space. But that was of no worry to me, I simply butted the next piece up against the first and screwed the drywall in place wherever I could find a 2x4 for backing.

What I didn't know then was that when a house is constructed the studs are built on either 16 inch or 24 inch centers. This means that when you hang a 48" wide piece of drywall, the edge will land in the middle of a stud. But the key is, you need to start on the right side of the wall. In my case, I had started on the wrong side and since the wall was 11 feet long, it meant my studs would land at 1, 3, 5, 7, 9 and 11 foot centers. None of those lengths can be equally divided by 4 feet. Had I started at the other end of the wall, my studs would have been found at 2, 4, 6, 8, 10 and 11 feet. All I needed to do was cut one foot off the last piece of drywall and every other edge would have joined on a stud.

By not joining the sheets on a stud, the joints now have no support and vibrations will cause the plaster mud to crack. Trust me, that is a mistake I will make only once! For those of you who have done drywall work, you know it is a laborious and taxing job and definitely not one you would ever want to redo from scratch!

Relationships though probably hold the greatest examples of trial and error and learning from our mistakes. We just were never given the playbook for how the other sex thinks. Guys love to joke about the flab they have hanging over their belt line, but how many times do you think it will take a guy to learn not to pinch that bit of flab on his significant other and state "maybe you should think about cutting back on the brewskies". And women, how long did it take you to learn that when washing dishes, if you want the back of the plates washed as well as the fronts, you're probably just going to have to do them yourself!

Like George Bush said "Fool me once.... Shame on you. Fool me twice....d'uh... we won't get fooled again". Okay so maybe some people aren't capable of learning from their mistakes!

Vision and The Ark

I first found the Ark searching the Internet while recovering from my broken arm, leg and back. Oddly enough, my fall actually motivated me toward moving forward again with my life instead of staying stagnant where I was. Although I enjoyed paramedic work, the job had begun to grow stale and I was feeling less and less challenged. Falling off of that cliff reminded me that tomorrow is not necessarily guaranteed and if I really wanted something there was no point in waiting. I knew succeeding in being self-employed in a field (team building and leadership) few people understood would be a monumental challenge and would require hard work and sacrifice. But I also had the confidence in myself that I was up for the challenge. I had just fallen 32 feet from a cliff, knocked myself unconscious, broken my arm, leg, and back, and hiked myself out to find help while still carrying a full climbing pack. Once I was healed, I figured that if I had the tenacity to survive a fall and recovery of that nature, I could handle the trials and tribulations of being self-employed!

This is the cliff I fell from. Monique is on top preparing for a rappel.

Tomorrow is never guaranteed, so ACT TODAY!

Corporate Synergy was already in operation and I had hosted a few decent clients. My methods included outdoor experiential education and I had been using my log cabin and 51 acres. This site was exceptionally beautiful and had amazing cliffs for rappelling, but it also had a few drawbacks. First, there was the size of the cabin. The biggest room in the place was less than 300 square feet and couldn't accommodate any more than a dozen people comfortably. And the second problem would eventually be my neighbours. They hadn't made any complaints yet, but here I was running a commercial enterprise on vacation property. I knew once my operation expanded, resistance from my neighbours would increase. And third, this property was an hour away from Ottawa with a kilometer stretch of un-maintained, seasonal, single lane, private, rutted, gravel road. So although day trips from Ottawa were within reason, the distance was pushing the limit

So here was my first Vision. I wanted to find a large wooded property, close to Ottawa, with no neighbours, rocky cliffs for rappelling, and room to build a structure that could accommodate larger groups of people. Since I knew I'd need to sell my cottage to purchase this property I was also hoping to find something with waterfront, but that wasn't mandatory.

The first location I found was in Ontario near Calabogie Hills. It was over 200 acres, had the P-K Trail running right through it, and was just over 30 minutes to downtown Ottawa. But when I went to visit it I found it to be a dense cedar forest with no elevation changes, no cliffs, an abundance of swamps, and deerflies by the thousands! My dogs and I were literally chased off the property by the assault of flies. There was no way I'd be able to bring a group of corporate executives to a site like this.

The next site was in Quebec about 35 minutes from the city and was absolutely beautiful. It was well over a hundred acres and had 100's of feet of shoreline. It contained a mature hardwood forest and was rocky with lots of elevation changes. There were no cliffs on the property, but there was plenty of room available to create a manmade rappel tower. Initially I thought this would be the perfect setting for both my home and the new Corporate Synergy retreat. I was so excited I could barely sleep.

But then I began to get a weird feeling about the site. The real estate agent knew I wanted to place an offer but he wouldn't return my phone calls. In the meantime I kept visiting the lot and hiking around, envisioning how and where everything would go and how great it all would be. Finally, I was able to corner the agent in his office and the truth came out. Apparently the land was owned by a gentleman who had just recently passed away and had bequeathed the property to his children. The one brother wanted to sell the land and divide the money, but the sister thought the family should hang onto it. They were in a deadlock with neither side prepared to change their stance. Also there were some issues with a legal right-of-way through the property that separated this land from the road. The agent was hopeful everything would be resolved, but I could tell from his posture that there would certainly be no positive changes in the near future. So my search continued...

It was becoming apparent that waterfront properties with large acreages were an exceptionally rare commodity. I had to expand my search and simply find everything I was looking for with the exception of a lake. The new search revealed a property with the following description: "164 forested acres with 6,000 square feet building (designed to be a solar home) +900 sq ft shed. Building is partially finished, (framing, metal roof, room divisions and window). Access to a small lake in Crown Land at rear of property and a view of two other lakes. Extremely private, easy access. 95% of electrical and plumbing for propane roughed in." The ad stated the property was 40 minutes from Ottawa and the vendor was asking $99,500. A photo accompanied this description and it basically looked like a barn settled in an overgrown field back-dropped by a forested hill.

"The Ark" as it appeared in the first year. With "security" like this it's probably no wonder that we were robbed!

Perhaps this could be the place? I contacted the realtor and met him the next day in Wakefield. He drove to the property explaining to me the merits and history of the area. It seemed as though we were traveling down this rugged gravel road forever! We finally arrived at this dilapidated structure surrounded by garbage in a field of tall thistles and weeds. There was definitely no initial chemistry between me and this abomination of a building.

The siding hadn't been completed, yet the wood that was up had already discoloured. Only a few of the windows had been installed and the paint on the windows in place was peeling in layer upon layer. Indoors there was garbage strewn everywhere and an unsettling odor drifted about the place. Upstairs the sub floor was certainly far from level and the garbage theme had been maintained in every room. To the naked eye, this place was a nightmare one would certainly want to wake up from as quickly as possible.

This is a view from the rear. You can understand why I had so much trouble staying warm!

My mind's eye however saw something completely different. This was a 6,000 square foot building, which, once all the garbage was removed, would be a completely blank canvass. The possibilities were endless! The main living area, the "great room", would house the kitchen, dining and living rooms, and was approximately 30'x30'. This was 900 square feet of uninterrupted living space and the living room had a vaulted ceiling roughed in and a big bay window on the south wall. There were two front windows (of which one was broken and covered in plastic) pointing to the west.

In this photo I'm standing at the front of the house looking back. I'm in the living room, the kitchen is on the left and the dining room on the right .

The light in that room during the day would be phenomenal (look how bright it is in the picture). I could install wood siding to make it appear as though it were a log structure. I could install a fireplace in the middle of the west wall as the centerpiece of the room. I could build a daybed under one of the slanted windows for afternoons spent lounging in the sun reading. The broken window could be removed and a door installed that would lead out to a large cedar deck.

The kitchen and dining areas were certainly big enough that a center island could be installed to allow space for food preparation while still entertaining with guests. A sink could be installed in front of a window on the north wall to allow us to gaze into the forest while washing dishes. Another large slanted window on the south wall would almost lead us to believe we were dining outside while eating our dinner.

This could be the greatest "great room" ever!

Further back in the house divisions had been installed to allow for six bedrooms and two bathrooms. But one room could easily become a main floor laundry facility; and another room would definitely need to be assigned as my office. In the back, a wall could come down to turn two of the rooms into one enormous master bedroom, again complete with vaulted ceiling. Each room had ample windows (or space in the wall to install one), and each room had beautiful views of the surrounding hills and hardwood forests.

There was absolutely nothing downstairs (except a gigantic sawmill blade and the garbage of course). It was simply one big space measuring 100 feet long by 30 feet wide. Sixty percent of the siding had been installed and the possibilities were endless! I would probably only install one divider allowing for a spacious 2 car garage with the remainder being left as an open space to accommodate my corporate team building guests.

What most people who passed by probably saw as nothing more than an eyesore, I saw as the answer to my dreams and the fulfillment of my Vision. It was beautiful. Another friend of mine who could also see past the piles of garbage and rotting wood stated, "This place is going to be a palace". I knew then and there that this place was going to be the new home of Corporate Synergy. The owner of the property just happened to be onsite (creating more garbage!) and I walked up to him and told him I was willing to pay him his asking price.

In this photo I'm standing in the "garage door" looking toward the back. You can see the stairs leading up on the left behind the leaning pile of doors.

This came as somewhat of a surprise to the realtor as after having the property sit on the market for over a year, interest had suddenly developed. A day earlier he had shown it to another woman and he expected to receive an offer from her that afternoon. Thus the realtor advised the vendor not to comment on my offer and stated he would be in touch with me later that week.

Surprisingly, the other offer that came in was also for the full amount requested by the vendor, but unlike my offer it came with conditions. The other woman was not much of a carpenter and was requesting the owner stay on to complete construction. But unlike me, the owner knew the reality of what it would take to complete a job of this magnitude and preferred to simply wash his hands of the place entirely. So the place was mine, all I had to do was find a way to pay for it!

Mike Caldwell

One thing I had forgotten to mention was a few months earlier I had sold a share of my company, Corporate Synergy, to an individual who wanted to work in an outdoor, education related field. He had recently moved to Ottawa from Victoria, British Columbia and had some considerable savings he was willing to invest in the business. Offering to purchase this property was probably a decision I should have consulted with him first!

When he came to view the place he certainly didn't have the same Vision as me. He just couldn't see past the rotting lumber, piles of garbage, broken glass, fields of weeds, and the abandoned, broken down, rusted out bus.

This Ottawa-Carleton Transpo bus was supposed to leave with the
previous owner, but somehow he must have forgotten it...

To him, there was nothing appealing about this property at all and he wanted no part of it. Unfortunately, the property was going to be a substantial part of the business and it wasn't possible to be involved with the company and not be involved with the property. Fortunately, this was an example of my friend believing in me, even though he had trouble sharing my Vision. So, luckily for me, my friend offered me a fairly substantial, interest free loan for one year. I was to use this money to place a down payment on the property and clean it up enough to entice a legitimate lending institution to properly finance the property. For all intents and purposes, this property was now mine! All I had to do was take my first step down the road toward my ultimate goal.

And this is how any dream worth having begins; with a strong and focused Vision. The second Habit in Stephen Covey's "The 7 Habits of Highly Effective People" states that people need to 'Begin with the End in Mind'. This is what I was doing. In my mind this site was already a beautiful building on a manicured property. All I had to do was work backwards to see what my first/next step should be. If I was going to begin living there immediately I would need a room where I could eat, sleep and stay warm. Since there was an old woodstove and chimney already in the great room, and since 3 of the 4 walls were already in place this would probably be the best room to start with.

In my mind, this room would have oak hardwood floors, tongue and groove pine walls, and a drywalled ceiling. But behind that pine and drywall would be a vapour barrier, and behind that vapour barrier would be fiberglass insulation, within that insulation would be the electrical wiring and in some cases, plumbing. So the place for me to start and begin to work forward would be to install the electrical and plumbing. Under the oak floor would be plywood, and under the plywood, more vapour barrier. So now I knew what needed to be done first on both the walls/ceiling and the floor. Thus, the Vision component of my dream had done all it could do. It was now time to bring on the Energy, Attitude, and Resolve!

Part 2

Energy

As you can now see, Vision alone is certainly not enough. I can sit on my couch eating potato chips, watching hockey and envision myself 20 pounds lighter. But without expending some Energy, that goal will never be a reality. Of course, it's easy to see how difficult it is to lose weight while eating junk food and sitting on my butt, but this premise is just as true for any goal you have in mind.

Do you want to earn a million dollars? Do you want to find your soul mate? Do you want to build your own log cabin? None of that is going to happen simply by thinking about it. There is work to be done, and you're the only person signed up to do it. So what are you waiting for?

Inertia.

Webster's Dictionary defines inertia as "the property of matter that causes its velocity to be constant in the absence of external forces". In layman's terms this means that something will continue onward at its current speed and direction unless something else acts on it. This is great news if you are already barreling toward your present goal but it's not the best news if you are currently stationary or traveling in the wrong direction.

And this is where Energy comes in. But where will this Energy come from?

Energy is everywhere

Regardless of what or where you look, the entity or product you see in front of you is ultimately comprised of Energy. Allow me to prove this to you. We'll start really big and break everything down until it's as small as it can get.

The biggest thing I know of is the universe and the last I heard, it is ever expanding. Expansion requires movement and movement is kinetic Energy.

Within the universe we find our solar system. Within this system there are planets revolving (kinetic Energy) around a big star we call the sun (nuclear and radiant Energy).

Within this system, there is the Earth which is revolving and spinning and creating wind and waves. There's obviously tons of Energy here!

On the Earth, you'll find yourself. And there you are, breathing, pulsing, moving, emitting heat... Right now you are full of chemical, potential, thermal, and kinetic Energy. Your body is comprised of organs, which are made up of tissues, which are made of cells built by atoms. At the very basis of it all, if you ask a quantum physicist "what happens when you break down an atom?"

She'll tell you "Energy!"

That's it. If you break anything or everything down into its absolute smallest components, you'll find but one thing and that is Energy. By now we all know just how much Energy is released if we split a plutonium atom. The atom may be small, but it can certainly pack a punch!

Now think back to your high school physics lessons. What is the one thing you probably remember learning about Energy? Energy can be neither created nor destroyed, but it can change from one form to another. Think of a book perched high up on a shelf, what sort of Energy does it possess?

Potential Energy.

If this book then falls off of the shelf, that potential Energy is transformed to kinetic Energy. When it hits the ground, all of its kinetic Energy is immediately transformed to radiant, thermal and sound Energy. These energies continue to travel on until they are transformed into something else.

So if something as simple as a book sitting on a shelf can transform Energy in so many ways, what is stopping you from accessing and utilizing the abundance of Energy that is around you right now? Look around you, what forms of Energy are there buzzing right beside you? I'm sure for most of us there is electrical Energy, radiant Energy, mechanical Energy, thermal Energy, light Energy, sound Energy, chemical Energy, not to mention all the microwaves, radio waves, cell phone waves, etc.

Just imagine if you could see all the Energy around you right now. You wouldn't be able to see a thing. Your entire world would be awash in bright, white light. All you have to do is figure out how to take advantage of the Energy that is all around you.

The Internal and Infinite Life Energy

When most of us need Energy, what do we say? "I need a coffee." Or, "I need a snack." Coffee contains caffeine which is a chemical that enhances the metabolic release of Energy within us. Similarly, snacks contain carbohydrates which when broken down in the Citric Acid Cycle produce ATP which our bodies can use for Energy (hey, maybe that biology degree is paying off after all!). But that is only one form, chemical Energy, which your body can utilize. Think back to some of the times when your body was energized without you ingesting anything at all.

Think back to a sporting event you may have attended. Since I live in Canada, hockey is the biggest event I usually go to watch. Regardless of the team you are rooting for, what happens to you when the home team scores? The majority of spectators leap to their feet shouting don't they? And when they do that, what happens to you? You suddenly feel entirely alert and energized. Why is that?

When the home team scores, the supporter of that team accesses his own personal Energy and with a scream and a jump, releases that life Energy out into the environment. For living things, there is no more valuable form of Energy than life Energy. It is this Energy that separates the living from the nonliving. And without getting too religious or philosophical, there is no more powerful Energy in the universe.

I don't think scientists have been able to identify the source or the nature of this life Energy yet, but there is no doubt that it exists. And similar to the splitting of an atom, or the power of a black hole, its potential is nearly infinite. A black hole is a collapsed star that only takes up a point in space, but has a gravitational force so strong that not even light can escape. Your life Energy is characterized in much the same way. It doesn't take up much room, but its potential is limitless.

It is this Energy that is being made available to you at that hockey game. But that is not the only example of life Energy transferring between living things. Think about some of the people in your life. There are those that take Energy and those that emit it. We all know somebody who is a literal Energy sponge. After 5 or 10 minutes with this person we are completely exhausted and drained. Conversely, hopefully we also know people who have the exact opposite effect. After we leave this person we feel energized and alive.

Ray Zahab running across the Libyan desert.

I'm fortunate enough to know a person who completely epitomizes this phenomenon. His name is Ray Zahab and in March of 2007, he and two of his friends finished a trek that saw them traverse the entirety of the Sahara Desert, from the Atlantic Ocean to the Red Sea, a total of 7,500km (4,660 miles) in 111 days. Ray and his friends ran an average of 70km (44 miles) per day, the equivalent of two marathons, through the sand, heat, cold, and windstorms, day after day for close to four months straight.

What enabled Ray to succeed at this journey? Was it the strength of his legs? Or the power of his cardiovascular system? Needless to say, Ray is one tremendously fit individual who trained hard and ate well in preparation for this epic journey. But physical strength alone is not enough to succeed at a task of this magnitude. Ray certainly had all the components of V.E.A.R., but it was his ability to access and utilize his life Energy that guaranteed him his success. Ray is the type of person who gives off so much Energy all the time that I wouldn't be surprised if you could see him glow in a perfectly dark room.

Ray is a personal trainer and a motivational speaker. This is an awesome combination for his clients. Regardless of their fitness goals, Ray inspires within his clients the confidence that they can do it. Seeing Ray's accomplishments is one thing, but after speaking with Ray, you leave feeling empowered and believing you too can accomplish anything you set your mind to. This is the power that exists when that life Energy is transferred.

Life Energy transfer isn't limited to human interactions though, it is also available in other forms. I grew up in Hamilton, Ontario and remember training for track and field running on the city streets. I was a decent runner and didn't mind running, but if given a choice I would ride my bike instead any day. Back then I would run for 30 to 40 minutes at a time and return home completely wiped out.

But then one summer, my parents took us camping up near Georgian Bay. I wanted to return to school that September fast and strong and continued my training through the summer months. I remember my first run out of the campground and onto the gravel roads and trails. At first I was worried because Parry Sound is much hillier than Hamilton and I was expecting the hills to tire me out. But much to my delighted surprise, I cruised up the hills like they weren't even there. Running on the flats was effortless, and the downhills were nothing less than pure enjoyment. I ran and ran and ran with no desire to ever return to my tent. I couldn't believe the Energy I had.

But where did it come from? I wasn't eating or drinking any differently. I certainly wasn't sleeping better on the ground than I was in my bed at home. It was the life Energy that was all around me. In the city, life Energy is at a premium. Sure there is tons of Energy all around but it is chaotic and conflicting. It isn't the pure juice of life Energy. Plus there is all that asphalt and concrete. It doesn't give any Energy at all, asphalt and concrete are only sinks that absorb it. But on the trails and gravel roads of Parry Sound I was surrounded by trees, grass, plants, animals, and insects. Everything around me was alive and, just like those fans at the hockey game, giving off Energy. All I had to do was open myself up to absorb it.

The bottom line is that you never have a "lack of Energy". Because not only are there infinite levels of external Energy, your life Energy also gives you all the Energy you could ever possibly need. All you need is the desire or motivation to access it.

Think back to one of the most draining days of your life:

- Maybe this was a work related day where you had to skip your breaks and lunch and still work 4 hours overtime to get the job completed.
- Or maybe it was a taxing day with the kids and your family, dropping one kid off at his soccer game just in time to pick your daughter up from dance lessons, just before your car's scheduled oil change appointment.
- Or maybe it was a spring cleaning "incident" in your house. You only meant to put away a few of your winter clothes but the next thing you knew rugs were hanging out on the line, windows were being washed, items were being boxed up for Goodwill...
- Or maybe after months of training, you finally finished running your first marathon or triathlon...

(And again, I'm serious here. Put the book down for a minute, lay your head back and close your eyes. Try and remember and relive the most exhausting day of your life.)

....

Okay, so hopefully you've pictured this day in your mind and are feeling appropriately exhausted. If you are anything like me, after a day like that I like to grab a glass of wine and a book (which I have no intention of reading) and lay on the couch. I take a sip of wine, lay my head back on a pillow, open the book up across my chest and close my eyes.

Ahhhh, finally I (you) can relax. Picture yourself laying there, your stresses of the day are finally slipping away and you can feel yourself begin to relax. You are just on the verge of nodding off to sleep and there is a knock on the door.

You're not expecting anybody and you certainly don't need a new vacuum cleaner or new religion! If it's important, they'll come back another time. Just as you close your eyes, the knock on the door returns, but louder this time. Your car is in the driveway, the lights are on in the kitchen and dining rooms, so they must know you are home. It would be rude not to answer it.

Your body is rebelling though. Your brain is telling it to sit up but it won't listen. You just don't have the energy to move. So you enlist the aid of gravity. Instead of sitting upright first, you roll your legs off of the sofa, ending up with your knees on the floor and elbows on the cushion. With a deep breath you get one foot underneath you then the other. Garnishing the last of your energy reserves, you stand upright and slowly make your way to the door.

"This better be important" you half tell yourself and the door. You can't believe how tired you are. "Has the door always been this far away from the couch?" Ensuring you have your best "evil eye" at the ready, you turn the handle and open the door. And who do you see standing on the other side of the threshold?

It's Ed McMahon wearing a huge grin and he is holding an enormous cheque with your name and a VERY large number on it...

How tired are you now??????????

Apparently you are not tired at all, because you are jumping up and down, screaming your fool head off. You are now completely awake and charged with Energy. But where did that Energy come from? Did you eat a nutrition bar on the way to the door? Did you down an extra large espresso coffee?

No, you didn't do any of these things. That Energy was in you the entire time. All you needed was that cheque from Ed McMahon to trigger it. But was that cheque the true source of the energy. Was it the only thing that would have worked?

What if it was your brother on the other side of the door that surprised you with a visit after spending a year overseas in some crazy war?

What if it was your husband on the other side of the door and you found out he wasn't "out for beers" at all? Rather he was surprising you with a dozen roses and that new car you have always dreamed of having.

There are literally dozens of things that could re-invigorate you after a long, hard day like that. So if all of these external factors can catalyze the release of that life Energy within you, doesn't that prove that the Energy is there and that it is real? And now that we know that Energy is there, do we really need Ed McMahon to knock on the door to unleash it? You would think there must be a way to access this Energy internally and on our own.

There is, but it's not often an easy thing to do. Frequently it involves conjuring up your Vision to truly motivate yourself for wanting that Energy, and it may also require a little assistance from Attitude and Resolve. But there are a few tricks you can use.

Brainwashing Can Be Fun

People always think "brainwashing" is a bad thing, but it can be used for good too. What I'm talking about is a conditioned Pavlovian response. In Pavlov's initial experiment, he conditioned a dog to salivate every time the dog heard a bell ring. The dog was trained to believe a piece of meat would be provided every time the bell rang. Salivating in a dog is a normal, natural response to the acquisition of food. Salivating to a bell ringing is not. But over time the dog was conditioned to link the two stimuli.

You can do the same thing to yourself! You can probably use meat and a bell if you like, but conditioned salivating isn't going to help you reach your goal. Associating music with Energy is.

Last year I competed in a 54km cross country ski "race". Although it is defined as a race, my main goal was simply to complete this 5 hour long winter endurance event. Since I was going to be out there so long, I borrowed my wife's MP3 player and programmed the music I liked into it. I'm a fan of classic rock so I had added a bunch of stuff from Led Zeppelin, Eric Clapton, Jethro Tull, etc. But I also added a few dance club songs that used to get me out on the dance floor back in university. You know, songs like "Pump up the Jam" and "Wiggle it".

Normally I would never listen to music like this while working in my workshop or anything, but I thought it might be fun to listen to while I was skiing. So there I was skiing along, enjoying myself while listening to Cream play "White Room", but the next song that came on was Ton Loc's "Funky Cold Medina". I couldn't believe it, from out of nowhere my Energy level shot through the roof. My legs were moving faster, my arms were moving faster, my head was bobbing to the rhythm. All my little aches and pains were gone and I felt terrific. It was like magic.

The only time I ever listen to "dance club" music, is when I am in a dance club! I had always been with my friends, I've usually had a couple of drinks, I was relaxed, having fun and usually dancing. While that song was on I was never tired, worried about work, school, or money; everything (at that precise moment) was great! So, while out racing through the Gatineau Hills, my mind blocked out the wind and the cold, the burn in my legs and the tightness in my chest. Rather it focused on the serotonin rush previously associated with "Funky Cold Medina".

It is that easy and it works every time. Regardless of what I'm doing or how I'm feeling, every time I turn on Ton Loc, my brain releases serotonin and norepinephrine, just like every time Pavlov's dog heard the bell ring his salivary glands released saliva. Although this conditioning occurred to me by accident, you can purposefully condition yourself the same way.

Every day, take 10 or 15 minutes to purely enjoy yourself. Maybe you might want to dance, or maybe you would prefer to look at old photographs that remind you of good times that made you happy. Then all you need to do is associate those happy feelings with a sound (music) or a scent. Every time I visit "farm country", the smell of the horses reminds of the great times I spent visiting my great grandfather on my uncle's farm.

Whatever works for you... Try your own experiment. I'm not a behavioural psychologist, so I don't know how long conditioning generally takes, and I'm sure it's different for every individual. I just know it works.

But conditioning is a process that takes some time to put into place. There are a couple of quicker methods you can try. First you can simply try using your Visioning skills. Just think back to a happy, Energy filled time in your life. If you have a good imagination and can place yourself back in that situation as fully as possible, it is quite likely those feelings of joy and Energy will return with them. Or maybe you just want to imagine opening your front door to find Ed McMahon and his big cheque on the other side!

If your imagination isn't all that good right now and that is something you're actually working on, then try this little trick. Instead of walking to your car or into the office, try skipping. That's right, why not skip instead of walk? Do you really think you can continue with low Energy and a negative Attitude if you're skipping?

Probably not.

In fact, although skipping is probably the best, any form of movement is better than staying immobile. Just think about what you look like when you're in a low Energy state. When I picture myself this way I am usually sitting down, hunched over, shoulders dropped, head and eyes low. But as soon as I raise my head, I start to feel better. If I pull my shoulders back I feel stronger still. Straightening my back gives me more Energy yet. And if I can break the inertia of not moving at all, once I'm up and skipping, I have all the Energy I need. And just as inertia can hinder one from moving in the first place, once that movement has started, it can be quite difficult to stop.

So really, with all this new information and with these new techniques, can you really use not having any Energy as an excuse?

The Law of Attraction

There is a top selling book and movie on the market right now called "The Secret". The premise of this book is that through the ages a "secret" has been passed down from one successful person to the next. But the authors of this book feel "the secret" should no longer be kept a secret and should be shared with the world. I've been meaning to write to them and tell them that they are too late, as "the secret" has already been exposed.

In 1981, my great-uncle Frank G. Thompson published "Success is an Inside Job" with Diliton Publications Inc. and in Chapter 24 on page 139, you will find "The Law of Attraction". This "law" is what "the secret" is.

Simply put, the Law of Attraction says "that which you think about most will be drawn to you", or "thoughts become things". In "the Secret", author Jack Canfield, Chicken Soup for the _____, states how he used the Law of Attraction to draw the National Enquirer to him to promote his first book and attain the grand launch he needed. Jack cites the Law of Attraction as being the driving force behind earning his first $100,000 and his first million dollars.

I have seen first hand the Law of Attraction and don't for a second doubt its power. But unfortunately I think

The Secret falls short in that it fails to tell the whole story. If you read The Secret you are lead to believe that just thinking about or wishing for something is enough. Similar to my previous chapter, The Secret speaks of the importance in having clarity of Vision. The clearer your Vision is, the more likely it will be drawn to you.

Apparently there are quantum physicists who believe that the electromagnetic waves your thoughts create in your brain travel outward indefinitely through space. These waves travel and travel until they unite with waves (thoughts) of a similar pattern and these "like" waves are then attracted or drawn together. Thus the more you think about and visualize something, the more wavelengths you send into the universe, and the greater the likelihood of your thoughts attracting the desired thing.

You may be like me and be a little skeptical of this premise. Although I may be the king of skeptics, I must also admit that I've seen the Law of Attraction in action and I know it works. I have held two incredible jobs that I never even applied for! I never applied to work as a raft guide on the Coppermine River. In high school, my friend Scott and I simply bought Paddler Magazine subscriptions in order to attain the ballots necessary to enter a draw for a canoe trip down the Coppermine. Then he and I would talk about it and dream about the experience and all the adventures and sights we would see. I never lost that dream and one day the owner of Arctic Waterways called and offered me a job on that very river!

Similarly, when I returned to Canada from Colorado, I desperately wanted to relocate in Ottawa, but lacking the ability to speak French created significant roadblocks that inhibited me from securing employment here. Then, one day "out of the blue", the manager of the Ottawa Air Ambulance Base called and offered me the position of Ottawa Paramedic Supervisor. This is actually a funny story as I wasn't actually supposed to be offered the job that day.

The vice president of the helicopter company was speaking with the nurse manager of the Sunnybrook Base Hospital program. The VP asked the nurse if she had any recommendations for the ambulance base supervisors. She gave him a few names and knowing the Ottawa base would be the flagship base of the program, recommended me for consideration there. Both the VP and the nurse manager speak English, while the Ottawa base pilot manager is Francophone with only basic English communication skills. Somehow "interviewing" me was lost in the translation when the VP spoke with the base manager, and instead of an interview I was simply hired on the spot. Keep in mind I never formally applied for that job in the first place!

How's that for the Law of Attraction?

But sadly, this process isn't as easy as it sounds on the surface. Sure I wanted to live in Ottawa and dreamt about it every day, but it's not like I graduated from high school, moved into my parent's basement and day-dreamed about the perfect job until the phone rang. The full story involves me:

- dropping out of university to go to school for ambulance work
- but returning to university the next year to finish my degree
- working my way up to paramedic partner with the ambulance service I worked for
- deciding to risk everything and leave my job for training in Colorado that probably wouldn't be accepted in Canada
- finding work with a fire service that not only gave me management experience, but the time and resources to pursue a Master's Degree
- deciding to leave Colorado and return to Canada not knowing whether I'd ever be able to find work

- arriving in Canada at a time when ambulance services were in a hiring a freeze
- staying resilient and creating a job for myself doing a diabetic research study with Sunnybrook Hospital
- meeting as many people as I could there and building relationships (including the one with the base hospital nurse manager)

And then, "from out of the blue", the Law of Attraction made me an "overnight" success. This is why I am writing V.E.A.R. now, most books don't tell you the whole story. The National Enquirer's promotion of Jack Canfield's Chicken Soup for the Soul didn't make Jack a millionaire. He made himself a millionaire. I have no doubt the Law of Attraction has played a role in his success, but that was only one piece of the puzzle. First Jack had to have a Vision of his book, then he needed the Energy to write it, he had to have the right Attitude that his book would succeed, and then he had to have the Resolve to stick with it after so many disappointments. It wasn't until he succeeded in all of these steps that the Law of Attraction brought the National Enquirer and his first big break to him.

> The Law of Attraction doesn't work independently; it is simply one piece in the overall V.E.A.R. process

You have to be careful though, because the Law of Attraction brings to you whatever it is you think about the most. Those are the thought waves spreading out into the universe. So if you're thinking about getting that perfect job or finding your perfect partner, that is what will be attracted to you. But what if all you think about is your lack of money, or all the "losers" you continue to date. What do you think is attracted to you then?

That's right, negative thoughts are just as powerful as positive ones, perhaps even more so. This is why it is so important to remain positive and optimistic. If you are a "glass is half empty" type of person, you'll never succeed in filling that glass completely. Sure you may be experiencing financial woes right now. Trust me I know all about money problems! But instead of focusing on how poor you are, you need to focus on the solution.

How is worrying about your debt going to help you? We all know that stress has negative consequences on your health. It can raise your blood pressure, create ulcers, increase your risk of heart disease, weaken your immune system, cause insomnia... Plus when has worrying about a problem ever fixed it? Now I'm not advising you to forget about that problem. For example, if you are financially strapped I don't advise you "not to worry about it", just apply for another credit card and keep spending!

Certainly not, I'm saying don't worry and stress about it, rather focus instead on a solution and do the best you can to get excited about that solution. There are basically two ways to solve financial woes: 1) spend less, and 2) earn more. These are the things you need to be thinking about. If you do this I assure you strange things will begin to happen. From seemingly out of nowhere you'll begin to find ways of saving money. Things you absolutely need will go on sale. A friend will offer you their old TV the day after yours breaks down. Someone will offer to purchase that camera you never use any more. You'll be asked to work some overtime at work, or maybe even be given a promotion.

Before you know it you'll be back in the black again. But if all you do is worry about your problems and think about having "no money", then "no money" will be drawn to you. This is when you need to replace the brakes on your car right after you installed a new transmission. This is when your office starts laying people off or making cutbacks. Positive thoughts bring positive results, negative breeds negative.

Don't underestimate the power of this "secret". My Uncle Frank spent 15 years on the pro wrestling circuit even though a bout with polio left him paralyzed for a year from the waist down. In his later years, he walked with a cane and in pain. But using the power of "the Secret" my uncle vehemently asserted he could find a parking spot right in front of any store, on any street, at any time of year. And no, it wasn't because he had a handicapped parking permit! Whenever he left his home, he would simply visualize the store and the street and an empty space right in front. He would then drive straight to that spot, never doubting the space would be open, available and waiting solely for him.

The Law of Attraction and The Ark

Unfortunately for me, I didn't clue into the power and the ways of "The Secret" until about four years into the construction of the Ark. Right from the beginning I knew and told everyone that building a 6,000 square foot home with no skills related to construction would be an uphill battle. I knew I would be faced with every trial and tribulation imaginable. I often stated that "Murphy's Law" (if something CAN go wrong, it WILL) should be changed to "Caldwell's Law". But although I hadn't formalized the V.E.A.R. process yet, I always knew that I possessed Vision, Energy, stubbornness and determination. I always believed that where there was a will there was a way.

If you believe in the power of the Law of Attraction, then you can just imagine with all my negativity, the type of "luck" that came my way!

Mike Caldwell

Not every aspect of building a house can be considered fun. Since I took possession of the property in February, I had to start the building process during the coldest month of the year. If I wanted the house to retain any heat at all it needed to be insulated. But before the insulation could go in, all the electrical wiring had to be in place. This is a job that unfortunately requires a certain degree of dexterity, and is usually not something that can be done while wearing gloves. My hands would literally freeze during that task. I would allow them to get so cold that I couldn't flex my fingers any more. Then I would simply stick my hands right inside the fired woodstove until the circulation returned. I would simply repeat these 2 steps all day long.

But jobs like that weren't any fault of "the Secret", they were simply rotten tasks that needed to be done. However, when I first purchased the property there was an abandoned, full sized, 1970 Ottawa Carleton Transpo bus broken down and sunken into the clay of the backyard. I certainly didn't have any use for this pile of rubbish and asked the previous owner to take it with him when he left. He completely understood and agreed as part of the sales agreement that he would ensure its removal and disposal. But as soon as we signed the agreement, I told my fiancé Monique that he would never move it and it would turn into one of my biggest headaches.

And guess what? I was right!

The guy never made any attempt to move it at all. Every time I spoke to him he would give me one excuse after another. The main problem was that we had plans to be married in that backyard and my fiancé didn't think a rusted out, broken down bus was the proper way to decorate the place. So I had to pay a local garage with a monster tow truck and flat bed to haul it out, all the while maintaining my negative thoughts on how difficult this task would be.

When I told the tow truck operator what he was faced with, he assured me there would be no problems at all. He'd hauled far bigger equipment than a city bus. But I remained skeptical and brought all my negative Energy down on that poor tow truck operator. His plan was simply to back his flat bed truck up to the front of the bus, set up his winch and haul the vehicle up onto the bed. Easy as pie...

After a great deal of difficulty accessing the axle of the bus (as it was sunken into the clay ground), the flat bed was eventually aligned and the winch cable set in place. The switch was thrown and the winching process initiated. The cable creaked and the motor groaned, the operator stood confidently nearby, and I stood there knowing this would never work and I would never be rid of this eyesore! And sure enough, "SNAP!" went the cable. The bus never budged, and the winch cable now lay on the ground splintered in two.

OC Transpo bus on the flatbed with tow truck and cables at the front.

Luckily for me though, the operator was a firm practitioner of V.E.A.R. He could see my bus on his flat bed and he wasn't going to give up until this job was done. (He definitely had an Attitude, although I can't really say how positive it was!). His next plan was to back the flat bed right up to the front of the bus, and then back his heavy duty tow truck to the front of his flat bed. He would then run his TWO tow cables over the flat bed truck and haul the bus up onto it. With these larger cables and with there being two of them, I started to believe we may actually see success on this day. And sure enough, despite some resistance from the bus, it eventually surrendered and was hauled into place and out of my life forever.

I literally have dozens of stories similar to this one, stories that should never have even been stories in the first place. Like the bus episode, had the previous owner simply taken the bus with him as he had promised, a second thought never would have been given to the matter. But I had to be negative and stress about the whole situation, and thus brought all this drama onto myself. My biggest expenditure of negative Energy though had to be related to finances. Right from the beginning I was in way over my head. Unfortunately, the biggest thing I inherited from my parents was their stress over money.

When I sold my house and cottage, and secured the private loan from my friend, I had the means to purchase the property, but nothing more. I couldn't afford any electrical wiring, plumbing supplies, lumber, drywall, windows...anything! My thoughts were that although this hurdle would be a huge challenge before me, I would have the perseverance and cunning to prevail. Sadly I was correct on all accounts. The hurdle was even bigger than I could have imagined, and it would take every ounce of my perseverance and cunning to succeed.

I had hoped that given my great credit history, and (at that time) stable paramedic income, that a bank would be more than willing to provide us with some form of construction or home equity loan. But not so. There was always some reason which caused us to be denied. Most banks had 10 criteria for lending money and we would always meet 9 out of 10 of those criteria. Some banks loved our property but couldn't lend to us because we were located in Quebec. Some banks loved our property but wouldn't loan to us because we were off the grid. Some banks loved our property but wouldn't loan to us because the house wasn't 95% complete. Some banks loved the property but wouldn't loan to us because we were zoned agricultural. And the agricultural bank loved our property but wouldn't loan us the money because we didn't have any cows...

It was all very frustrating and you'll learn more about how we overcame these complications in the Attitude and Resolve sections. But the bottom line is that I always said nobody would lend us the money, so nobody did.

You can just imagine how tight the "finances" were with no firm backing from a lending institution. It was all I could think about. I would lay awake late at night worrying about it, dream about my problems all night, only to awaken early to re-commence the worrying. All I could think about was how much credit card debt we were piling up, and how much everything was continuing to cost. We never caught a break...

When it was time to drill the well, the inspector told us how it was unfortunate we didn't contact him 2 months sooner. A new law had just been implemented that stated if we didn't have 10' of topsoil before the drill hit bedrock, then we would need to install a special $2000 seal around the head of the well. Of course, we only had 6' of topsoil and had to pay $2000 on top of our $1500 well for a seal we wouldn't have needed if a) we would have called 2 months sooner, or b) hired another well drilling company that didn't have this new seal technology yet!

Mike Caldwell

There are a multitude of other stories of financial woe as well, but these I will save for the Attitude and Resolve chapters.

Extreme Energy and the Ark

The prevailing importance of Energy however is not found within the individual stories. Energy's main role was within the mundane existence of day-to-day life during the construction of the Ark.

I moved into the Ark in the heart of Canadian winter. The back third of the house was covered in a thin sheet of plastic. The exterior walls of the remainder of the house were simply 8 inch pine boards with ¼ inch gaps between them. The floor to the main living area was constructed of 2x4's with wide gaps opening to the frigid cold outside below.

Initially I believed creating a warm haven for myself would come easily. I would simply install drywall on the back walls of the kitchen and dining room as well as a temporary door exiting to the rear of the house. Despite my improper installation of the drywall, this step was performed with relative ease.

Then I would need to simply place fiberglass insulation between the interior wall studs to block heat escape from that avenue. But unfortunately before the insulation could be installed, the electrical wiring had to be in place. There were two problems here: 1) I had never done any electrical wiring before and had no idea how to do that or what the "Code" was and 2) before I could install the wiring I had to know what the final layout of all three rooms was going to be. Where would the fridge, stove and dishwasher sit? Where would the entertainment center be located? What and where would the lighting and switches be?

The most important thing about living in an off-the-grid home is not how it is going to create electrical Energy, but how it will conserve it. One of the most overlooked Energy drains in a home are those from "phantom loads". These are drains on power that appliances use when they are not in use. Did you know your television and stereo are both using electricity while sitting idle in the corner? There is more power being used there than just that little green light.

To give you an idea on just how important this issue is, I'll give you examples from my home now that it is running "normally". In the winter months, our house uses an average of 200 amp hours of power at 24 volts over a 24 hour period. These 200 amps goes toward running our refrigerator, lights and television in the evening, my computer during the day, the well pump, circulating pumps for our heating system, the fan for our oil boiler and the AC-to-DC power inverter for our off-the-grid power system. When not in use, our entertainment center (32" colour television, stereo system and satellite TV receiver) uses 2.5 amps of power per hour. So if we were to not watch TV or listen to any music all day, my entertainment system would use 60 amps of power! Right now our home is only using 200 amps to run everything within the place. This one phantom load alone would increase our energy consumption by 30%! Keep in mind, every amp of power we use, we have to find a way to generate.

In order to prevent these phantom load losses, I had to know in advance where these phantom load appliances would be placed. With this knowledge I would be able to place switches on the electrical outlets where these appliances would be plugged into. By turning the switch off, I cut all power to that appliance and save those phantom load losses. (If you would like to make the same savings in your home you can simply plug your phantom load appliances into a power bar and turn the power bar off when those appliances aren't in use.)

So I had to show a little patience here. As much as I wanted to be warm, I had to make sure I did everything right the first time. I had to buy books entitled "The Complete Guide to Home Wiring", research code restrictions in my province, and use my Vision to determine the final layout of the rooms.

Installing wire in subfreezing temperatures is not an easy task. Electrical wire is very stiff and doesn't like to bend in these conditions and since a fair bit of dexterity is required, it's tough to do a lot of the work while wearing gloves. Installing all the metal electrical boxes and feeding all the wire through the studs was a very laborious and time consuming process. I could see the final Vision in my mind but I didn't want to go through all of these painstaking steps to get there. It was ironic how much Energy I needed to find within myself to install the wiring for the power I needed to energize my house!

Eventually though, I met with success. The wiring was in and the insulation and vapour barrier quickly followed. The only remaining gap that needed to be filled before I could warm the room was sealing off the floor. Again this should have been an easy and straightforward task. The 2x8 floor joyces were down and strapped with 2x4's. This was a very solid floor and simply needed a vapour barrier covered by 4x8 sheets of plywood. Even working alone and having to carry over 30 sheets of 5/8" plywood up the stairs one at a time, the job should have taken less than 2 or 3 days.

Unfortunately though, "Ron", the original builder of the home knew even less about home construction than I did! Although he had assured me he had been building homes for 30 years, he certainly hadn't learned any lessons in the relationship between wood and water. In order to save money, Ron had used lumber that had been milled directly from the property here. There is nothing at all wrong with this and I think it's a great idea. But this is a hardwood forest here with very few pine or spruce trees and Ron decided to go with poplar as his main construction medium.

Poplar is an interesting wood as it is relatively soft and easy to manipulate when fresh cut, but once it dries it becomes as hard as steel. One of the problems with its drying process though is that the wood tends to bend and twist as it loses its moisture. When Ron installed the poplar 2x4 subfloor, the wood had been freshly cut and was still dripping wet. Although it was probably quite heavy, it was likely fairly easy to work with. But now dry, it was my turn to deal with it. Many of the boards had twisted and a few of them had curved upward. When I laid a sheet of 4x8 plywood on the floor, it rocked back and forth from corner to corner.

There was no way I would simply be able to lay the plywood sheets on the floor and screw them in place. Since this was going to be a "home", the floors had to be flat, and since oak hardwood would be the final application, the floors had to be perfectly flat! Thus, before I could screw the plywood into place I had to identify any and all of the high points and with an electric planer, plane them down. (I ran a portable gas generator with a long extension cord to power my tools- one day the plastic covering cracked because it was so cold in here!).

The problem with this was there were nails deep into the wood at 24" intervals. These nails had to be removed before the wood could be planed. But since a nail gun had been used on soft, accepting poplar, the nail heads had sunk beneath the surface of the boards. And once the wood dried, hardened and shrank, the nails were now extremely resistance to being removed. Some individual nails would require 5 or 6 different tools and close to 10 minutes for their removal. Keep in mind I had nearly 900 square feet of flooring to contend with in this room alone!

So try and picture this: Spending an entire day on your hands and knees fighting to remove nails before planing down rock hard poplar decking. Constantly placing and removing sheets of plywood to determine the level, before finally being able to install a sheet. All of this was being done in sub freezing temperatures while handling all metal tools. The days are long and exhausting. But eventually it becomes too dark to work and there is nothing left to do but make a pot of spaghetti on the Coleman stove and climb into a freezing cold sleeping bag.

Morning arrives earlier than you want and you open your eyes to see the task before you. The saddest thing is that the view you have now is not that much different than the view you had yesterday morning! You have to get up because you have to go to the bathroom, but this is the part of the day you dread most. You're warm in your sleeping bag now, but you know from experience how cold those clothes beside you are. And the temperature of the toilet seat and the cold wind blowing through the outhouse is still fresh in your mind as well!

You're not out of bed yet and you're already exhausted! Wouldn't it be nice if Ed McMahon came knocking on your door right now? Or better yet, how about Bob Villa or Mike Holmes? Unfortunately, NOBODY would come knocking on this door at this time of year. So if it was Energy you needed you would have to find it yourself.

The first thing I did to survive these days was to remove the enormity of my task from my mind.

How do you eat an elephant? One bite at a time!

How do you build an Ark? One nail at a time!

I couldn't focus on EVERYTHING that had to be done; I only focused on the first thing that was on my list. Okay, I had to remove those 2 nails and plane that one board. That's not so hard. I don't feel quite so overwhelmed now. Little by little progress was made. And with Monique only coming up once a week, I was able to get excited through her as after a week of labour, she would notice some significant progress.

My next conduits of Energy were Fred and Maple, my two border collies. They must have been as cold and tired as I was but they weren't showing it. After sleeping on my mattress tight beside me for warmth, they started every morning with a huge show of enthusiasm. They were so happy and excited that if I allowed it, their Energy was infectious. Before I knew it I was laughing and energized and making jokes about the stiffness of my socks.

Fred and Maple keeping one another warm in front of the partially constructed daybed.

My third strategy for accessing Energy was simply reverting back to my Vision. Sure I was currently living in nothing more than a shell of a home, but one day it would be a palace. Seeing this clearly in my mind's eye was all I needed to once again brave the cold air, the cold clothes, the cold toilet seat, and cold hands. With this Vision I had all the Energy I would need to meet the demands of the day.

Life at the Ark, Not as Easy as it Looked!

Without being able to access this Energy, there is a very real chance I may not have even survived this project. In the Acknowledgements section of this book I thank my friend Al. Al was great, he and Paul were always here when my back was to the wall and I really needed help. Paul mostly helped me because he is a nice guy and being from Newfoundland, helping one another is a part of his culture. Al helped because he too was a nice guy but he also thought I was living the dream life!

I was self-employed in an outdoors related field, I had a beautiful and loving fiancé, and I was living the life of a pioneer, building an off-the-grid home with my own two hands. Al would often tell me how lucky and great he thought my life was. Although I certainly appreciated these sentiments and gained Energy from them, I warned Al to be careful for what he wished for and explained my life was not nearly as exciting and exotic as it looked on the outside.

In my third winter at the Ark, Al was able to find out first hand what I meant by that! Monique and I had been given a free vacation in the sunny south, and Al agreed to stay at our home, look after the dogs and work on any projects that interested him.

During his week here, Al experienced the following "adventures":

- On one occasion, Al's truck slid right off the road into the ditch
- On another occasion, the ice wouldn't allow his truck to make it up the hill and was so slick that he was able to shoulder the vehicle

from one side of the road all the way over to the guard rail on the other side.

- The running water had been installed at this point, but there was no heat in the house other than the woodstove in the great room. The pipes froze while we were gone and the plastic fitting going into the toilet's holding tank broke causing water to leak everywhere.
- We had begun installing the downstairs woodstove but had only friction fit the chimney. That came crashing down in the middle of the night leaving Al to wonder who (or what) was messing around downstairs!
- In an attempt to stop further pipes from freezing, Al began installing insulation around all of the water pipes. At one point he was up on a ladder, and for reasons still unknown to him, the ladder collapsed, leaving him hanging from a plastic pipe within a 12' high ceiling.
- The firewood we had ordered for the woodstove the previous winter wasn't cut and split until late that fall and was delivered dripping wet with sap. It resisted burning, and when finally forced to burn refused to give off any heat. Al was generally unsuccessful in ever warming the great room and experienced a chill throughout his entire stay here.
- Al prefers staying up late and sleeping late in the morning. I prefer going to bed and waking up early. Fred and Maple had learned the latter and refused to allow Al to stay in bed much past sunrise.

Monique and I returned from our vacation, tanned, re-energized and invigorated. But upon arrival, Al was but a shell of the man we had left. He was pale, cold, and sick as a dog. This had been the longest week of his life. What he thought was the ideal lifestyle was more a test of his fortitude.

Unfortunately, unlike me, Al didn't have the little "victories" of pulling a nail or planing a board to energize him. He certainly performed whatever task he could while he was here, but most of his time was spent trying to get warm. And given none of these tasks were bringing him any closer to HIS Vision, he didn't get the same sense of satisfaction that I did.

Al admits that during that week, the highlight of his day was taking Fred and Maple for their afternoon walk. What he probably didn't know was it was during this time that he was opening himself up to absorb their Energy and that of the wilderness around them. Sadly, instead of absorbing that same Energy in the early morning, he actually expended more of his Energy fighting it off!

Bell Canada Sucks the Energy from my Soul

The last example I will share (although there are certainly dozens and dozens more) is the ordeal I experienced having a telephone installed here. When I first placed my offer on the property I contacted Hydro Quebec to see how much it would cost to bring hydro into the place. I explained about our rural setting and the fact that we were 2km from our nearest neighbour and 2km from the nearest Hydro/telephone pole. Hydro informed me that an installation of this magnitude would cost somewhere around $45,000. Okay, that was fine, I guess we'll go with living "off the grid" then.

I then called Bell Canada to learn how much it would cost to install a telephone here. Their response was approximately $75 (that's no typo there, they said SEVENTY FIVE dollars). I argued with them and explained my proximity to my neighbours and telephone poles and shared with them the $45,000 quote I received from Hydro Quebec. But after a long deliberation and support from a Bell Canada manager I was assured the charge would only be $75. So I went ahead, was assigned a telephone number, and arranged for installation. Sadly I failed to get our agreement in writing...

On the assigned day, the Bell Canada technician arrived at the house in his pick up truck. Incredulously he asked if I was the one expecting to have a telephone installed. I stated that I was and he just laughed. He stated there was no way I could ever get a telephone line brought here, not at any price! He stated the land was too rugged and I was too far away from anything for an installation to be possible!

This was not good news, but sadly, due to my misuse of the Law of Attraction, it was more or less the news I was expecting. Fortunately though, this technician was wrong and installation would be possible. The only problem is that it would cost me somewhere around $40,000!

This is a great story, but you're going to have to read further into the book to see how it develops. It was the Law of Attraction that created this unnecessary hardship for me, but it was Resolve that got me through it. So you'll just have to wait until then to find out what happened!

Part 3

Attitude

Some people say that "Attitude is everything", but in V.E.A.R. it is only one quarter of everything. Nonetheless, Attitude is extremely important.

Many people start into a project predicting to fail. They believe the odds are stacked against them, and doubt that deep down they really have what it takes to succeed. Most times though, people believe there is "no harm in trying", so they put forth a minimal effort hoping to get lucky. If (and when) they fail, there's no shame or embarrassment, because "at least they tried".

But did they really? If I decide I want to bake a cake (and I'm not a baker), and refuse to look at any cake recipes, can I truly say I tried to bake a cake just because I mixed together a handful of flour, sugar, lard, and water and threw it in the oven for an hour to cook? No, if you truly want to bake a cake you need to do it right. You need to find the right recipe to suit the celebration and ingredients you have on hand. Then you need to follow that recipe to the letter. You need to mix the appropriate amounts in the proper order and then cook it at the specified temperature for the specified length of time.

If you follow ALL of these steps as concisely as you are able, THEN you can say you attempted to bake a cake. More than likely, if you used fresh ingredients and followed the recipe you'll be met with success. If for some reason the cake didn't rise, then you re-evaluate your process, analyze what may have gone wrong, and you TRY AGAIN! If you really want that cake, you certainly won't stop after one failed attempt.

"What lies behind us and what lies before us are tiny matters, compared to what lies within us" – Oliver Wendell Holmes

If a project is worth starting, then it is worth your complete attention and effort. If you are going to start something, don't leave yourself any window at all for failure. In many cases, I don't even recommend devising a "Plan B".

Last Christmas I was visiting my in-laws and telling my father-in-law all about Corporate Synergy, the motivational speaking and team building work I was doing. My father-in-law is a very pragmatic man and has worked his way up through the commercial roofing industry. Commercial buildings need roofs, and since my father-in-law is good at what he does, he has built a very successful enterprise. But nobody "needs" a team building facilitator or motivational speaker. When the economy is good and companies are doing well, I have the potential to be busy. But if the economy is poor and businesses are keeping their budgets tight, I may not work at all. And since I am somewhat responsible for my wife's happiness and security, my father-in-law simply asked me an honest question: "What happens if Corporate Synergy doesn't succeed?"

I have to admit, that question actually came as a surprise to me. I certainly know the reality of the business that I'm in. The nature of the work I do is very subjective and impressions can be fickle. I have never doubted that succeeding in this line of work would take a great deal of effort on my part. But to be honest, I had never considered that I wouldn't succeed in my dreams. My motto is "If it can be done, it can be done by me".

If it can be done, it can be done by me.

Other people have been successful in my line of work. Tony Robbins, Les Brown, Brian Tracy, Stephen Covey and others have all made fortunes motivating people to be the best they can be. What do these gentlemen possess that I don't? I'm educated, I have experience, and others have told me that I have a way of relating to people. There are certainly no obvious obstructions to my success. From where I sit, if I apply V.E.A.R. with all my heart and soul, success is inevitable.

However, it is important to be realistic. If I was 5'4" tall and dreamed of being a center in the NBA, how realistic would that be? "If it can be done, it can be done by me"... Are there any other 5'4" centers in the NBA? No there aren't. So maybe it can't be done, not by me, not by anyone. Of course there are always firsts for everything. People said a man would never walk on the moon and look what happened there!

Earlier in this book I told the story of Oprah Winfrey. Here was a woman who, early in her life, was not dealt a very good hand. But she was certainly able to turn things around in her favour. So what about you, what does Oprah have that you don't? In fact, it's probably fair to say that most people have a leg up from where Oprah started from.

So there you have it. Your new goal is to be "the most influential woman on the planet." (I understand for approximately half of you reading this book, that your first few steps will be countless reconstructive surgeries and hormone injections! But just humour me for a minute).

Is your goal of being the MOST influential woman on the PLANET truly that realistic? By definition there can only be one of these people and that spot is currently filled. And keep in mind you'll also be battling with Hillary Clinton, Condoleezza Rice, Wu Yi, and others for that title. I know, I know, I'm supposed to be motivating you here. Motivational speakers are supposed to tell people they can do anything they set their minds to.

Well that's how I'm a bit different. I'm a motivator who wants to actually increase your odds at success! Let's think back to the Vision chapter of this book. Remember that red Ford Mustang I thought I wanted? Use that process now to decide whether or not you really want to be "the most" of anything.

How much free time do you think Oprah enjoys? Can she just stop by McDonald's for a Big Mac anytime she feels like a greasy snack? How many people rely on her continued success? What will happen to all those people if she ever fails? And then there is the multitude of people like me! I must call her 20 times a day, hounding her to read this book and place it in the Oprah Book Club (okay, I'm just kidding, I'm lucky if I'm able to leave a dozen messages a day with her...).

My point is, somewhere in the back of your mind, you may have already considered these negatives. If this is the case, then your subconscious is going to be sabotaging your efforts all along the way. So instead of stating you want to be "the most influential woman on the planet", identify which aspects of that goal appeal to you. Perhaps you simply like to influence others. Is there a way of doing that without having to attain global domination? Sure there is; you could become a teacher, a coach, a team leader or a manager at work.

Perhaps it's not the influence, but the implied money that accompanies that degree of power. How can you improve your financial situation? You could get a promotion at work, or some training for an entirely different career altogether.

Maybe it's not the influence or the money. Maybe you're just looking for a bit of recognition. Why aren't you getting the recognition you feel you deserve? Do you really deserve it in the first place? What changes could you make in your life that would improve your profile?

Okay, take a second here and think of somebody you know who always displays a positive Attitude. Try and think of somebody who is so assured within him or herself, that you can't even imagine them failing...

(Seriously, put this book down right now and think of somebody! Get back to me when you've done it.)

....

For me, the guy I always think of is Muhammad Ali. Man, did that guy ever have an Attitude! Here are just a few of his quotes. Hopefully they'll inspire you as much as they do me.

- *"I am the astronaut of boxing. Joe Louis and Dempsey were just jet pilots. I'm in a world of my own."*
- *"I'll beat him so bad he'll need a shoehorn to put his hat on."*
- *"I'm not the greatest; I'm the double greatest. Not only do I knock 'em out, I pick the round."*
- *"I'm so fast that last night I turned off the light switch in my hotel room and was in bed before the room was dark."*
- *"It's hard to be humble, when you're as great as I am."*
- *"It's not bragging if you can back it up."*

In what arena are you an "Ali"?

Are there any arenas in your life where you are as confident as Ali was when it came to boxing? Maybe nobody can match you in a game of Charades. Or maybe nobody can bake a black forest cake to rival yours. Maybe you can disassemble and reassemble a Chevy big block engine in your sleep...

Most of us have that "one thing", where we have complete confidence. Sure you may acknowledge that somewhere in the world there is somebody who can tie a fly fishing fly better than you can, but there certainly isn't anyone in your immediate group of friends! Who catches the most fish, and who's the one who is always lending his flies? In your world, you are the greatest. You know it and everyone else knows it.

Give some thought now to some of the attributes that make you the best at whatever it is you do. Certainly you have experience in that arena. That experience has given you skills, knowledge and ability. But what is that one additional thing that makes you so good that everyone knows it?

Confidence.

It is because you are confident in your skill (as a Chevy big block engine guy), that when your buddy's car won't start, you say "pop the hood and let me take a look at it".

If you had experience, knowledge, skill and ability, but no confidence, you never would have stepped up and risked showing your potential ignorance. Once you fix that engine, everyone will know who to call when they are having car problems (sorry about that...)! And once you are identified by all your peers as "the car guy", your confidence will continue to grow allowing you to take more risks, learn even more, and become better still.

> Positive feedback causes even more positive results.

If you don't attack a project with confidence, your odds of succeeding are greatly decreased. Sports and the outdoor environment provide us with some of the easiest illustrations. When whitewater kayaking, it is imperative that you paddle with confidence. If you need to get to that point on the other side of the river, but paddle too timidly, the current will simply whisk you away, leaving you to flounder and search for another safe haven.

Other similarities exist in downhill skiing and snowboarding, rock climbing, and mountain biking. If you don't completely control whatever maneuver it is you're attempting, that maneuver will control you. This is true outside of sporting events as well. What happens if you're not sure how to bake a cake and you keep opening the oven door every five minutes to see how it's doing?

Your cake probably isn't going to rise is it?

What happens if your friends convince you to ask for a raise? You don't think you really deserve one, but to please your friends you go into your boss's office and half-heartedly ask for one anyway. Do you really think you can convince your boss you deserve a raise if you haven't even been able to convince yourself?

I honestly believe that "if it can be done, it can be done by me". Before attempting any task at all, I have to have 100% buy-in to that philosophy. If I don't, I know I'm leaving a window open for failure. So I simply close that window and begin my undertaking with 100% confidence.

Monique's Ironman Journey

Of course, you certainly need to be practical as well. A couple of years ago my wife Monique had some issues with her back. She didn't experience any sudden trauma or anything, but something in her spine slipped somewhere and she was out of commission and in considerable pain for close to three months. Once the pain fully subsided, the road back to complete recovery and strength was a long one. So in 2005 she began training for the Somersault Promotions 5km Women's Day Run in June of 2006. Her goal wasn't to win; she simply wanted to run the entire distance without stopping.

Although she was successful in finishing that event, she did admit that there were a couple of short sections where she needed to walk. But regardless, this experience buoyed her spirits and shortly afterward she was looking at accomplishing an even grander task...

Saying I was "surprised" would be too much of an understatement when Monique came to me and said she wanted to race an Ironman Triathlon in 2007. An IRONMAN! That's 2.4 miles of swimming, followed by 112 miles of biking and a full 26.2 mile marathon of running! That's quite a big step up from running a simple five kilometer road race.

When I asked her which Ironman she was considering, she said she thought the France Ironman would be nice. FRANCE! This is one of the most daunting iron distance races of them all. After a pleasant four kilometer swim in the Mediterranean, racers are taken up into the French Alps to cycle around for 180km. As you probably know, the French Alps aren't known for their "flatness". So here is a woman who wants to run 42km after spending the previous eight hours riding her bike up and down one of the largest mountain ranges in the world!

Like I said, I'm not one of those motivational speakers that assures a 7 foot tall Sumo wrestler that he can certainly be the world's foremost horse jockey. So despite wanting to support my wife, I didn't know if her attempting an Ironman was the best idea, and tackling the event in France certainly wasn't the best set up for success.

After speaking with Monique, I could tell her heart was set on this goal and I could see she had the Vision, Energy, Attitude and Resolve to succeed. So there was nothing left for me to do but support her. I learned that she was choosing the France event not so much for the race itself, but more so for the venue. Although racing an Ironman was her primary priority, second to that was experiencing a nice vacation with me and drinking wine in a picturesque locale.

Now I had something I could work with. After a quick Internet search I learned about the Vineman Iron Distance

Triathlon in Sonoma Valley, California. Although this certainly wasn't an "easy" course; it did have a couple of big hills on the bike leg, and few more substantial hills on the run, it certainly wouldn't be as arduous as France. Since the race was located in Sonoma Valley, the weather was guaranteed to be beautiful, we'd be near the ocean, and there would certainly be no shortage of wine to taste! Although Monique was initially disappointed about my views of the France race, after some of her own research, she began to grow more and more excited about Vineman.

I must admit that although I was always outwardly positive and supportive in her endeavour, deep down I had my doubts. Monique has a ton of amazing qualities, and many of those qualities would serve her well in a race of this nature and magnitude. But physically, I just didn't know if she was cut out for such an undertaking. She not only had a history of back related problems, but she was also the first to admit she wasn't built for running. Not only did she not enjoy running, but right from her first few steps on the road her heart rate would elevate through the roof and her breathing would be out of control.

But here is where ATTITUDE comes into play. She never once focused on the negatives or "what if's", rather she only focused on the positive and what she could control. She'd seen me race in iron distance events and she had seen men and women in far poorer physical health than she was in. So if they could do it, why couldn't she?

Monique hired a personal trainer and followed her instructions to the letter. If she was supposed to bike 40km with her heart within a set zone that is what she did. If she was supposed to follow that ride up with a 30 minute run, she did that as well. Monique's Resolve was incredible (but that story is for the next chapter!). One of her biggest secrets to success however, was that she didn't attribute her tenacity to Resolve at all. Rather, she simply approached each workout with a positive Attitude.

She never viewed her workouts as something she "had" to do. Rather, for the most part, her workouts were something she looked forward to. Training for an Ironman is a year long process as best. Many people train for 2 or 3 years before attempting their first race of this distance. If she had viewed every day as a chore, sticking with her regime would have been much more difficult. But instead of dreading her Monday evening swim session, she looked forward to it and the opportunity to reconnect and catch up with her swim buddies.

Her long rides and runs were an opportunity to escape the rat race of life. On the road she could forget all of her troubles and responsibilities. All she had to worry about was managing her form and controlling her breathing. She could also concentrate on how she felt and what all this training was doing to her physically. After just a few weeks of training, she began to feel that she had more Energy in every aspect of her day. On the scale she could see her weight coming down, and her muscles beginning to emerge. As her husband, I can assure she wasn't the only one noticing (and taking advantage of) these changes!

There were only a couple of areas where her Attitude faltered. It was her belief that she could not run, nor could she control her heart rate when she was out on the roads. She also didn't want to train with me at all. We are simply from two far differing genetic make ups. She has to train and work really hard simply to finish a 5k run, whereas I barely had to do any training at all prior to running my last marathon. It's frustrating for someone who has to work so hard for something to compare herself to somebody who can just cruise with minimal effort. Thus, it was difficult for me to really help her out in her run training. But finally one day I was able to arrange it so that I left a half an hour before her run, and since there is only one road to train on up here, I was able to catch her on my way back.

Self Imposed Mental Barriers

Since we live in the Gatineau "Hills", the gravel road leading to our house is not without changes in elevation. For the most part the road is gently rolling, but over a 5km stretch there are three significant hills to contend with. On this day, I was able to catch Monique just prior to her tackling the first of the three hills. Luckily she was open to some constructive advice and I helped her a bit with her body positioning, breathing, and cadence. She thanked me for the advice but warned me that the hill was approaching and that she'd have to walk and she'd resume what I taught her on the other side.

I suggested she forget about the hill altogether, and instead continue to focus on her form and breathing. She agreed to do so, and with my constant encouragement, she made it to the top of the hill without walking a step! She had never done this before! Although that hill was relatively short, it was the steepest of the three. The next hill wasn't as steep, but it felt like it went on forever. Monique told me she didn't think she could run all the way to the top, but she would concentrate again on her form and breathing and do the best she could do. Again, I kept yapping and encouraging her all the way and before she knew it she was cresting the top again!

She couldn't believe it. She was of the opinion that she couldn't run hills and would never be able to do so. After that last hill, Monique was definitely experiencing a "runner's high". Unfortunately, that high popped as we approached the last ascent. This hill was the mother of the previous two hills as it was just slightly shorter than the last one, and just slightly less steep than the first one. Monique assured me there was no way she'd be able to run the entirety of this hill, especially after running nine kilometers and besting two hills she'd never beaten before.

I was not there to argue with her; instead I just encouraged her to do her best. I got her to shorten her stride, lean forward, drop her hands, and focus on her breathing. With a couple kilometers of practice already under her belt, she was able to maintain her form with little effort and was able to focus solely on her breathing. And again, much to her disbelief, but not at all to mine, she crested the last of the three hills, not perhaps at a full run, but she was certainly not walking!

It was incredible. And from then on, she never had to walk any of those hills again. There was nothing physically different about her on that day than on any of the previous days before. The only roadblock to her success was in her mind. She didn't believe she could run any of those hills, so of course she couldn't! All I did was be there to share some of my Energy with her and take her mind off of her negative misconceptions. Following that day, with her newfound belief that she COULD run those hills, she simply did it. The intimidation was gone and her confidence was high.

Do you currently have any "hills" in your life you're not succeeding at? Not because you physically can't but because your mind won't permit you the opportunity to succeed? Think about it, and figure out where those negative beliefs are coming from and what you can do to abolish them forever.

Race Day

You're probably still wondering what happened with Monique and her quest for Ironman glory?

The weather in Sonoma Valley is usually fairly consistent. At night moist ocean breezes blow in off the ocean to cool the entire coast. In the morning, the sun's heat evaporates all this dampness creating layers of fog and cloud. Around noon all the humidity is gone leaving glorious heat and bright sunshine in cloudless skies. Early morning temperatures are in the low to mid 60's (Fahrenheit), stabilizing around 70 through the morning and into the 90's through the afternoon.

Race day was a different story however. As I entered the water for the race at 6:45am the sun was already peeking over the hills. There was no fog and there were no clouds. Emerging from the water an hour later, the temperatures must have already been nearing 80 degrees! It was going to be a long, hot day.

Just as I was emerging from the water on my way to the bike transition, I saw Monique's peacock blue swimsuit (she was easy to spot because all the other racers were wearing wetsuits) just beginning her second lap. Unbeknownst to me, she had forgotten to take one of her anti-gas tablets and had been swallowing more air on this swim than she usually does when not faced with the pressures of racing. So when she finally emerged from the water, she was experiencing some tremendous abdominal cramping. She was able to take an anti-gas tab in the transition zone, but still started the 112 mile bike leg with some considerable pain.

Apparently the cramping and pain lasted with her for about an hour. The sun was now beating down on all of us at full strength, and despite the heat and sweating; Monique was unable to take in any fluids. So this meant Monique had been exercising for nearly two and a half hours in the dry California heat without taking in any liquid or nutrients. People who race long distance triathlons frequently refer to the "fourth" discipline; that being fluid and nutrition intake. If a racer fails to keep their engine cool and fully fueled, they will suffer greatly before ultimately experiencing failure.

Monique climbing "Chalk Hill" during the Vineman Iron Distance
Triathlon

So Monique was definitely behind the 8-ball early
into the race. But once she got her cramping issues
resolved, she regained her positive Attitude and did a
personal inventory. There she was in Sonoma Valley,
competing in the race of her dreams, biking through valley
after valley of vineyards, and at last check there were still
people behind her! She decided she could either focus on
the negative and suffer all day, or she could focus on the

positive and enjoy herself in a race she traveled 4000km to compete in.

She didn't panic at all; she just went to work at replenishing her Energy stores and hydration levels. Apparently at one of the bike check points she must have looked worse than she felt because officials there made her stop and receive a dousing with a garden hose to cool her down. As usual, the wind picked up as the day progressed, and fighting a head wind, Monique finally made it to the end of the bike and into the run transition.

The run course was three out-and-back loops of some exceptionally hilly and rugged paved asphalt roads. I had had a great swim and a fairly strong bike. Knowing Monique was going to be facing more wind and heat than I had to, I expected I was probably a good two hours ahead of her. If everything worked out, I was hoping to run into and maybe run with her as I finished my final lap. But much to my surprise, as I was stopped at a checkpoint on my return leg to the transition, I saw Monique running toward me, looking relaxed, comfortable and happy. I was barely an hour ahead of her and it appeared as though she was having the time of her life!

We crossed paths two more times during the race, and both times she looked to be in good spirits and was able to tell me that she was still having fun! I couldn't believe it. I was so proud of her. I didn't know if we'd ever have the opportunity to attend a race together like this again and I wanted to do something special. So before reaching the finish line, I jumped off of the course and mixed in with the crowd. I took the timing chip off my ankle and went to the transition bag drop off to pick up my pre-swim attire. The sun was beginning to set and the temperatures were cooling dramatically.

About an hour later, Monique arrived to finish the second of her three laps. I knew Monique's knee was beginning to bother her, and with just over two hours remaining I was worried that if she couldn't run much more and was reduced to walking, she might not make the 16 hour cut off time. I tried to warn her about my time concerns as she made her way back onto the course for her final lap, but she just blew me off. She knew how she was feeling and what she was capable of, and wasn't worried for a minute about finishing the race in time.

I was still wearing my wet run clothes, and was dehydrated and beginning to shiver. But I was able to find a couple of reflective blankets which I made into a skirt and used to keep as much of my body heat in as possible. I then joined in with the remaining spectators, cheered in the last competitors, and waited and prayed for Monique.

With just under 30 minutes to spare I saw her through the dark make the turn around the corner. I quickly put my timing chip back on, dropped my reflective blankets, and joined her to run the last few hundred meters through the finish. Knowing the dedication and commitment Monique showed for this event made finishing with her the most joyous Ironman finish of my life. Monique too loved the entire experience and fully expects to try another and improve upon her time within the next couple of years.

Monique and I crossing the finish line in Sonoma Valley, 2007

Appreciation

I find appreciating what I have instead of lamenting what I'm missing goes a long way in contributing to maintaining a positive Attitude. How many of us ever experience road rage to some degree? I don't necessarily mean the type of road rage that results in aggressive driving, lewd hand gestures or actual physical confrontations. But just the every day stress and anger caused by driving in heavy traffic. Just think about how agitated your driving has made you in the past.

Now try and think back to one specific instance where you have been extremely stressed while driving your car. If you're like me, you probably have a hard time remembering a specific instance. Unless being stuck in traffic resulted in you missing a flight or you having to deliver your baby in the back seat, you probably don't remember a specific time that heavy traffic almost caused you to be late for a lunch date!

And seriously, 9 times out of 10, that is the "problem" you are worried about; being five minutes late for work, or five minutes late for a hair appointment or missing the start of your favourite TV show. How many times have you arrived somewhere completely stressed out only to find you're still the first to arrive or your appointment is running late? And the person on the other side of your interaction doesn't seem stressed about the new time schedule in the least.

So was it really worth it? Was all that stress and aggravation worth the quickened pulse rate and increased blood pressure? We are all guilty of this, but how do we let these petty annoyances get so far under our skin? Let's try another visualization exercise.

You and your spouse have dinner reservations and tickets for a concert afterward. But of course you leave the house running a bit late. You drive into the downtown core only to be faced with immediate gridlock. You keep switching from one lane to the other, but neither line seems to be moving. As you approach one particular yellow light, you pull into the left lane, placing you second in line to go through the intersection. As soon as the light turns green, you start to advance, but just then the car in front of you turns on his left turn signal!

What is he doing? Didn't he know he was going to turn left before he approached the light? And now why isn't he advancing into the intersection? He's just sitting there! And what's he doing? Is he talking on his phone? Finally the light turns yellow, all the oncoming traffic is making the most of their window of opportunity and the car in front of you only proceeds just as the light turns red. You can't move at all.

Your dinner reservations were for five minutes ago! By the time you park, get seated, order a drink (you definitely need a drink!), and order dinner, it's highly unlikely that you'll have time for dessert. What was supposed to be a nice night out is quickly turning into the night from hell! Why do you even bother?

Have you ever been in a situation similar to this? I'm sure we all have. But again, can you now remember any specific instances? In the end, don't these "nightmare" occasions usually work themselves out? What if we approached the evening with an entirely different perspective?

First, what if we weren't late leaving the house in the first place? What caused you to be late? Were you busy trying to decide which shirt best matched your pants? Or did you "need" to just water the plants quickly before you left? I guarantee nobody at the concert is going to be asking herself, "why did he wear a brown shirt with those pants, doesn't he know a navy shirt would have looked much better?"

And what if somebody is thinking that? Who cares!

But let's say you do leave the house late and you are stuck in traffic. You're with your spouse aren't you? When was the last time you and him/her had some decent alone time where you could talk? Here is a perfect opportunity. I'm sure you have plenty to talk about. What did you do today? What should you do for next summer's vacation? Do you have any ideas for some home renovations? Instead of lamenting being stuck in traffic, cherish this opportunity to share some time with a loved one.

And where was it you were going again? You were headed to a nice restaurant. In many instances in life, the anticipation is more rewarding than the actual thing itself. Instead of stewing about not actually being there, start visualizing the atmosphere you're about to experience. Why not get those salivary glands working right now? What are you in the mood for? Maybe a cream soup... Definitely some red wine... What entrée might pair itself well with a nice Shiraz?

Keep in mind, you are headed toward a nice meal. Okay you might be there at 7:15 instead of 7 o'clock. But the food is still going to taste as sweet. And you don't have to cook or wash any dishes. These are only the smallest things to appreciate. Let's broaden your perspective even further with an example from the Ark.

The Value of a Box of Screws

In order to purchase the Ark I had to sell my house and cottage and move into a shell of a building with only three walls, no insulation, no heat or running water. The Ark cost me $100,000 but I only made $50,000 profit from the sale of my two properties. Since I was purchasing agricultural land in Quebec, I wasn't eligible for any form of classic bank mortgage. But my previous business partner was willing to lend me $50,000 interest free for one year. So there, the Ark is "paid for". Now all I had to do was purchase enough siding, electrical and plumbing supplies, solar equipment, telephone poles, insulation, vapour barrier, drywall, flooring, furniture and fixtures to turn a 6,000 square foot sawmill into a home!

Where exactly was this money going to come from? I was only working as a part time paramedic now and since I didn't have a telephone there was no way I could be notified when shifts became available. Similarly, my personal business Corporate Synergy certainly wasn't flourishing without a telephone or fax machine. But "luckily" my credit was quite good and the credit card companies were more than willing to lend me all the money I needed. At 21% interest!

Now I'm really not reckless with money and I did have a plan. Although I was ineligible for a construction loan for a number of reasons: the home was off the grid, we were in Quebec, we were located on agricultural land, we didn't own any cows... (that was Farm Credit Canada's ridiculous excuse), I was told that if the house was 90, or 95, or 98, or 100% complete (I got a different number from every person I spoke with), we would be eligible for a full mortgage at the going mortgage interest rate. So all I had to do was race the credit companies to the finish line. If I could finish the house, before running out of credit to pay off my credit, we could secure a mortgage and live our lives with much less financial stress.

As you can probably imagine, over the four years it took to "finish" the house and secure our mortgage, we certainly experienced some stressful times. After the first two years, every couple of months I would be nearly ready to accept defeat. The money was all gone, the credit was all gone, but we still had bills coming in and debts to pay. I had no idea what we would do. But I always did my best to keep my Energy high, stay positive and show Resolve. And time after time, at the 11th hour I would land a Corporate Synergy contract, or we would receive some money for Christmas; something would happen that would buy me just a little more time.

There were times when things were darker than dark. I remember one time when I called Monique at work and asked her to bring home some milk and bread. In response, she told me to choose one. She only had the parking change left in her car, she had no money, and all our credit cards were over the limit. We could get the other item in two days when she got paid!

I even went to a bankruptcy lawyer for advice. Ironically, the house that no bank would touch was worth too much for us to be eligible for any programs or to even declare bankruptcy! The only option that seemed available to save us was to sell the property, pay off our debts, and start again with nothing. But luckily, being a proponent of V.E.A.R., I didn't have to submit to this option.

Through all of this I continued to support my foster child in India through the Christian Children's Fund. I promised myself when I was in South America in 1992 that if I ever had the means to support a child when I "grew up" I would. So the day I received my first paycheck from Canadian Helicopters in 1999, I enlisted with the Christian Children's Fund and adopted three year old Sujauddin from Calcutta.

When some of my friends found out that I was considering either bankruptcy or selling the house, and that I was still supporting a foster child they thought I was crazy. Many of them advised me to put a hold on my $30/month payments until I was in a better financial situation. And I must admit I gave it some consideration.

However, if I had an extra $30/month to spend what could I buy? I could buy a box of wood screws or two sheets of drywall. If I saved up for two months I could buy a bag of insulation or a gallon of paint. If I saved up for three months I could purchase a roll of electrical wire or a fixture for the sink... But if I kept sending my $30/month to Sujauddin, I would ensure that he had food, medicine, clothes, an education and shelter. How could I possibly trade these things in for a box of screws?

Whenever I started feeling sorry for myself, it was very easy to turn things around and realize how good I actually had it. Sure most of you probably take for granted having a gallon of milk in the fridge AND a loaf of bread on the counter. Granted there was the odd day when that luxury wasn't afforded me, but I never worried that there would never be a loaf of bread on my counter again.

Perspective

What was my worst case scenario? Well, quite frankly I could lose everything. I was approximately $150,000 in debt making monthly payments of close to $6000. The banks didn't care about my situation or my potential to make good. The only thing they cared about was their monthly interest payments and making more and more money. If I had to sell everything to make good on my debt, that was of no concern to them.

So let's say I did lose this battle. My land alone was worth $99,000 and by this time there was a 6,000 square foot "house" on it. Sure it wasn't finished, but it was 90% complete and what was in place was of the highest quality. In the real estate market at that time I probably could have secured $225,000 for the property, and definitely no less than $200,000. So if I did "lose everything", somehow I would walk away with at least $50,000 in my pocket! Okay, that's probably not the best return on my four year investment considering all the blood, sweat and tears I put into this place. But I would still have $50,000 in the bank, a Master's Degree education, health that is good enough to complete an iron distance triathlon, a beautiful wife who I love and loves me, and the companionship of the two best border collies on the planet.

For a guy who just "lost everything", my life really wasn't looking all that bad. Certainly if the worst case scenario were to happen, I would be justified in some respects to have something to complain about. Had I chosen a different path and taken the safe route of gainful employment, I would probably have had a nice house (built by professionals!), a new car, an annual vacation destination, good credit and some money in the bank. But that would have meant working for somebody else and playing by their rules. I much prefer being the person who dictates the way I live my life. If my choices work out, that is great, but if I fail I have nobody to blame but myself. So given the value I place on freedom, even in "failure" I can hold my head high because I was able to do things my way and on my own terms.

Aside from that personal satisfaction, I had an even better reason to appreciate the hand life had dealt me. Certainly by Canadian standards, a 39 year old male with good health and a Master's Degree has nobody to blame but himself if he does not achieve above average financial success. But those are by Canadian standards; again I prefer to think more globally.

I know many of us, myself included, frequently plead poverty. But do we really know what poverty is? The World Bank has a list of averages of the national per capita incomes for the world's top 208 countries. Only 75 of these countries have national average annual incomes that exceed $10,000! And with approximately 6.5 billion people living on this planet right now, over 4 billion of these individuals earn less than $2 per day. When North American's consider their financial status with a world wide perspective, I think you'll agree we're all doing fairly well. There are actually 1.2 billion people on this planet who would have to put in two full months of work simply to afford the cover price of this book! With this perspective, I really can't allow myself to feel too bad about only having $50,000 to put down on a new house and the means and opportunity to earn considerably more if I simply put my heart into it.

Plus at 39 years old, I still have my whole life ahead of me. With an estimated life expectancy in Canada of 80 years, I'm not worried at all about having to start again almost from scratch. I've barely made it to the half way point of my life! However, if I was born in Malawi,

Mozambique, Rwanda, or Zambia, there is a very good chance I'd be dead already since the average life expectancies in those countries is less than 40 years of age!

So it basically all boils down to perspective. Let's think about you being late for your dinner reservation again. Is your life really so terrible that it deserves all that stress, anger, and anxiety?

Where are you again?

Sitting in a climate controlled, comfortable automobile in a country that is ranked with one of the highest standards of living on the planet.

Where are you going?

Out for a nice meal where they'll bring you all the fresh bread and water you could ever eat and drink for free! A waiter will bring you a menu, where you will choose from any number of sumptuous dishes that somebody else will prepare and bring to you. And of course you'll be consuming this off of the finest tableware in a most pleasant environment.

How many people living in a village in the heart of the Sahara or Serengeti have an evening like this available to them as an option?

I wasn't able to find any hard numbers here to answer this question, but I'm guessing not very many!

How do you think these people would view your dismal mood and negative attitude simply because you're going to be 15 minutes late for a pleasure they have no hope of ever experiencing?

It's all about perspective. Next time you find yourself frustrated and all in a dither, step back for a second and reassess. I'm sure if you look at your situation from a distance and with some objectivity, it won't be nearly as bad as you currently think.

Your Attitude is linked to your Energy. If you are always carrying around a negative Attitude, then you'll only attract negative Energy. But if you maintain a positive Attitude, positive Energy will surely flow in your direction.

Maximize the Potential of a Positive Attitude

Although this premise is also true with Vision, Energy, and Resolve, don't simply use Attitude as a tool you pull out of your toolbox when you think it's needed. A positive Attitude isn't like hammer you pull out whenever you need to drive a nail. A positive Attitude should be adorned every morning before you put on your pants!

I do a number of motivational presentations to people learning to run or looking to improve their distance or time. I tell them that before or during a race or training session, they need to have a positive attitude, not judge themselves, and appreciate their health and the environment they find themselves in.

Frequently though I am asked the question: "What can you do though when you are in a race or even a training event and find yourself at rock bottom?"

My honest answer to that is sometimes there is very little you can do to immediately improve upon that situation. But I always follow that answer up with a question of my own.

"How did you come to be at rock bottom in the first place?"

From my experience I've never been skipping along, whistling my favourite tune only to turn a corner and find myself in the bowels of depression. No, the transition from 100% happy to 100% depressed is usually a multi-staged progression.

I may be happily skipping out to my car only to be met with a parking ticket. Then driving to my appointment I may be cut off by an inconsiderate driver. Then construction tie-ups make me late for an appointment. And when I arrive at my destination I find I missed the meeting entirely. THEN I have to meet my running group for a training session.

How motivated and positive do you think that workout is going to be?

For most of us, myself included, we're going to be in a miserable mood. Sure we'll do the workout but we're not going to enjoy it, and there's no way I'll be idling chatting with anybody. If I do speak, it will only be to bitch about what a terrible day I've had. Who wants to listen to that?

Certainly, even if you had the inclination to conjure up a positive Vision or borrow some Energy from the group around you, the likelihood of your success is minimal. This is one of those times when your hammer just isn't big enough to drive this particular nail! Trust me, I speak from experience. On page 37 there is a picture of me giving a presentation at StatsCan in Ottawa. Do you know what is happening to my car while I'm standing there?

That's right, some jerk is giving me a $25 parking ticket!

Certainly that is maddening in and of itself, but what is more maddening is that I was parked in a 2 hour parking zone. Do you know how long I was parked there?

One hour and fifty minutes!

Do you know what time I arrived at my car?

I arrived at 1:45 pm.

Do you know what time it said my ticket was issued to me?

That read 1:50pm!

So not only had I not broken any parking violations, but the issuing bylaw officer lied about the time I was ticketed! I was furious. First I called the City of Ottawa and tried to fix this situation immediately, but there was nothing they could do. Then I called Monique, simply to yell and vent and release some of my frustrations.

Then I left the complex to run some errands. It was a very windy day and somebody's garbage can had blown into the middle of the road. Again I started yelling and cursing.

"Why can't people control their garbage cans?"

"There are people walking on the sidewalk. Don't they see a garbage can blocking traffic in the middle of the road? How hard could it be to simply grab it and place it in a driveway???"

"People are so inconsiderate and stupid!"

But then for some reason, I took a step back and looked at myself from a distance. What the heck was I doing? I had become a raving lunatic. What was wrong with me? Sure I had just been dinged for $25. But how was that going to irrevocably alter my life?

It wasn't. But how was my current mood going to alter the rest of my day? At this rate the rest of my day was guaranteed to be miserable. There was no way around it. And how was yelling and screaming and throwing hissy fits going to benefit me in any way?

It certainly wasn't. And do you know what I did at that point?

I laughed. I was alone in my car and actually laughing out load. I had just left giving a motivational talk feeling energized and uplifted. I had just advised 70+ people to hold a positive attitude and appreciate the good in their lives, and now what was I doing? I was behind the wheel of my car screaming at a garbage can.

You've got to admit, that's a pretty funny picture.

And with that laughter came a new boost of positive Energy. Instead of focusing on the negative I turned to appreciate what the day HAD offered me:

- I just finished a great motivational presentation. People came up to me afterward to shake my hand and share their stories with me.

- I had filmed the presentation to submit to an agent I was hoping would represent me and assist in bringing me more business.
- I was driving my 2 month old Honda Odyssey minivan. I know it sounds geeky, but unlike the '65 Ford Mustang, this really is my dream vehicle.
- And it was windy. Man was it ever windy! My new wind turbine at home must be spinning and making power like crazy!

Okay, so maybe I'm out of pocket 25 bucks. This is actually a pretty funny story. Maybe a story like this will find a place in my new book!?!?

In this instance I was lucky. My bad mood was relatively new and hadn't descended any lower than my anger over receiving that unjust parking fine. I caught it in time and was able to turn my negative Attitude around. In fact, I was even able to turn my "Anger Energy" into a more positive form of Energy through my laughter.

The moral of this story is simply to catch yourself when developing a negative Attitude as early as possible. We're certainly not robots programmed only for happiness and joy. Emotions are what make us human, and negative emotions are a component of that mix. However, we do have a conscious choice whether we wish to follow that negative, destructive path or make a U-turn and follow a more positive and productive road.

Strategies for Securing a Positive Attitude

There are two strategies that I most like to employ. First I try to start every day with a positive mindset. New days bring new opportunities. Even days that I know are going to introduce problems I welcome. Experience has taught me that problems can frequently turn into learning experiences, adventures and opportunities. Corporate Synergy was supposed to simply be an Outdoor Experiential Education company, but thanks to an economic decline I now have great fun doing motivational speaking and now I am the author of a book!

Each morning I try and wake with the same energy and enthusiasm as my two border collies. I look at the upcoming day with the proper perspective: I'm warm, dry, healthy, and fit. I live in a beautiful home with my beautiful wife. There is food in the fridge and a computer on my desk. I live in Canada and my opportunities are without limit.

These statements are true each and every day. Each morning I can either focus on them and create a positive outlook for the day, or I can think about the tax bills from Revenue Canada, the broken transformer for the radiant heat downstairs, the cracked windshield in the car, or all the work I need to do with my new website.

Which early morning mindset will ultimately end the day with the more positive results? If all I focus on are the problems facing me that day, why would I ever want to even get out of bed? But if I begin the day confident and positive, these "problems" are no longer problems at all, rather they are challenges life has presented to me to prove and strengthen my Resolve. This is what life is about. Bring it on!

> Don't focus on "problems", rather, attack those "challenges" with energy and enthusiasm.

I also don't worry too much about what other people think about me. I have my own goals and expectations for myself, and these were developed with the consideration of the people who matter in my life. If somebody else thinks

I'm wasting my education and experience because I'm no longer a paramedic or firefighter that is their problem. Some people think that because there are thousands of people in this country who want to work as a firefighter I'm disrespecting them and myself for not following that career path.

However, I don't look at it that way. For me firefighting was a tremendous experience and an adventurous part of my life. But then, that chapter came to an end and it was time for me to move on. If somebody else wants to harbour negative Energy about me, that is their decision but I'm not going to let that bring me down.

People in Canada can also be a little on the conservative side, and especially people in Ottawa. For some reason it's no longer in our nature to show our emotions. As you've learned, I do my best to stay positive and have as high an Energy level as I can. I always do my best to greet people with a smile and when they ask "How are you?" I respond with "Fantastic" or "Great" or "Couldn't be better". Although they don't say it, I quite often see them question in their eyes "What's this guy so happy about?" like there is something wrong with me!

What sort of people do you know that seem to be happy most of the time without significant cause or reason?

Children! That's right. They don't tend to worry or stress and they are always running around singing and screaming. But for some reason when an adult is described as "acting childish" it's a negative thing!

On the contrary, whenever somebody tells me that I'm acting like a child I thank them for the compliment!

For some reason there are people in this society now who actually feel guilty for feeling happy and thus try to hide these feelings from the world. I find it strange that so many people work so hard to earn money to buy the things that make them happy. But then, once they have those things they feel guilty for enjoying them!

Why do people always feel they have to act so cool? It's now been three months since I bought that Honda Odyssey minivan, yet I still smile every time I get behind the wheel. I absolutely love this vehicle and get excited every time I drive it. Yet I have other friends who save for years and spend stacks of money on a sports car or half ton pickup and when I ask them "So how do you like your new car?"

They say "It's okay".

"Okay????", you're driving a car that can go zero to sixty in three seconds and all you can say is "it's okay"? What's up with that? Don't be afraid to grin from ear to ear while saying "it is completely AWESOME! Every time I get in this thing it scares the crap out of me. I never thought I'd ever be in control of that much power."

Show some pride, some enthusiasm, some excitement. If you asked a four year old what he thought of his brand new bright red fire truck, I can guarantee he won't respond with "it's okay". Once you learn to appreciate what you have and where you are at in life, take it one step further and learn how to truly enjoy and be happy about those things and accomplishments.

Part 4

Resolve

Although Resolve is the last stage of V.E.A.R., it is certainly not the least important. You can have a terrifically clear Vision, all the Energy in the world, and a strong positive Attitude, but if you can only hold those three qualities together for a day or a week, you are doomed to failure.

Resolve is your ability to stick with something through not only the rough times but the good times as well. What do I mean by that? You probably think it's easy to stick with something when the going is good, and to some degree it is. But you need to be careful about choosing to settle for something less than your overall Vision. Jim Fannin in his book "S.C.O.R.E for Life" provides a great metaphor for what I'm talking about here.

Jim tells the story of a hungry cheetah. She hasn't eaten for days when she comes along a herd of impala grazing in a field on the Serengeti. The cheetah stays low and appraises the herd. Near the middle she sees a healthy young buck and this is indeed the filet mignon of the group. The cheetah envisions that particular impala as her lunch for the day but knows it to be a worthy adversary. She crouches low and circles around the perimeter of the field, doing her best to get as close to her prey as possible.

Once in position, she waits and is patient, never taking her eyes off of that tasty lunch. Unknowingly, the targeted impala moves through the herd a little closer to the cheetah, and when the time is just right, the cheetah explodes into the masses. There is chaos as the impala scatter. Everyone is darting to and fro and bumping into one another. But the cheetah never loses focus. Just in front of her a small yearling loses his balance and falls. The cheetah leaps over this helpless victim. Another impala, this one an elder of the herd also cannot deal with the stress and submits. But again the cheetah hurdles this fallen prey. In the mind's eye of this cheetah, there is but one impala on this plain and that is her only target.

The impala is strong and agile though and darts this way and that. The cheetah is kicked once and is momentarily stunned. But she simply shakes her head and continues in pursuit. Eventually the impala tires and begins to slow, enabling the cheetah her final pounce. The prize is hers just as she envisioned it would be.

Have you ever had an eye on a prize but failed to acquire that prize because a lesser impala fell at your feet? I'm sure it has happened to all of us and there are times when this is not a bad thing. Let's go back to the beginning of this book when I said I wanted a 1965 Red Mustang Convertible. Later I decided that I didn't want it bad enough to make all the sacrifices and commitment V.E.A.R. would require. But what should I do if one day I found out my neighbour had a 1968 blue Pontiac Firebird hard top in his barn that he would sell to me at an extremely reasonable price?

If I am honest with myself, am I ever going to get that '65 Mustang?

No probably not.

What is it about that car that I like?

Well there is the raw power aspect of the machine, the lines of it, and the fact that it is a vintage classic.

Does a '68 Firebird share any of these qualities?

Well certainly it does! Is it a Mustang? Well no. But is it "close enough"?

In this case a '68 Firebird is close enough. I would absolutely love this car. I would fix it up, wash it, wax it, deep clean it, and only drive it on the sunniest of days. I would take great pride in owning that vehicle.

If the opportunity arose, would I ever trade it for the '65 Mustang?

In a second! But until that day arrived I would certainly have no regrets.

In an example like that it is important not to show too much Resolve. If I hold out for that one particular car, with my current priorities, I will never succeed in owning any vehicle with pride. But in settling for "second best", I still have the opportunity to feel great about my situation.

However, I can't follow that same philosophy for the things that hold a higher priority in my life. My top 4 priorities are: 1) my wife, 2) my health, 3) my house, and 4) my career. It's important for people to identify what their priorities are and learn to act on that information. Would I give Monique my kidney if she needed it, even if it might diminish my health? Yes I would. Would I sell the home that I built if I had to to stay with my wife? Yes I would. Would I put an end to Corporate Synergy and get a full time job if it was necessary to stay with Monique? Again, yes I would.

Would I leave Monique if it meant I could earn more money doing what I do in Toronto? No, I wouldn't leave Monique or my home simply to make more money. Would I work day and night, sacrificing my health if it meant I could make more money? No, because again I wouldn't sacrifice my health for money nor would I want to take away any time I already spend with my wife.

Establish your priorities BEFORE you expend Energy sticking with your Resolve.

By asking questions similar to this it's easy to establish your list of priorities. But what is tougher is actually acting on them. How many people say their significant other and their health are the two most important things in their lives? But how many of these people never take a vacation and work weekends and 12 hour days simply to earn even more money for an even bigger house and a newer, more expensive car? That car and big screen TV aren't going to make you any healthier or bring you any closer to your spouse (at least they shouldn't!).

You need to figure out what is most important to you and then develop a plan where you can use your Resolve to act on it.

The finished living room of the Ark, oak floors, pine walls, stone hearth with woodstove.

Over the past four years, building this home has been very close to my Number 1 priority. It held this position for a number of reasons. The Vision Monique and I shared for this finished project was our dream home. This would be our sanctuary and the place where we raised our children. It would be so much more than a simple house. Since we've attempted to build this place with every luxury we could afford, it would not only be our home but our vacation retreat from the world.

Mike Caldwell

The neat thing about building your own house is that you can design it to your own specifications. Monique and I are both tall, so when I built the kitchen island and counters I created them slightly higher than that found in your standard kitchen. Similarly, when a local hardware store was selling their floor model of a "Cleopatra" soaking tub at a terrific sale price, we scooped it up. Monique and I both love the feeling of warmth provided by wood and so instead of installing sheetrock in the living area, I installed 8" tongue and groove pine. In the bedrooms, we determined where the beds would be located and placed a light switch low on the wall so the light could be easily closed right from the comfort of the bed.

So, this home meant greater happiness for both my wife and I. And when a couple is happy, their relationship is better.

The Ark would also serve as the headquarters for my business. Initially I had planned to host adventure race clinics and corporate retreats here. The forests that surround us are perfect for teaching the skills of map and compass navigation and there are also enough cliffs for teaching rope skills. I built trails that are perfect for mountain biking and with a lake at the back of the property and the Gatineau River only 4km away, paddling instruction was easy as well.

On the corporate side, I left the downstairs area wide open to provide us with a 2,000 square foot meeting facility. I built challenge and high ropes courses in the woods and installed a climbing wall on the outside of the house. After Monique and I hosted our wedding here, we also realized that we had a wedding venue that would be high in demand.

As I mentioned earlier, we were doing all of this with almost no money. Any money that did come in, had to go right back out to at least pay the 21% interest on our already existing debt. But the only way we could possibly survive all of this was to get the house finished so we could secure a single low interest mortgage loan. Keep in mind, my health is also a top priority of mine and carrying that much stress certainly wasn't good for it!

So you can probably imagine why finishing this place was such a HUGE priority for me. Along the path to completion, it seemed as if every three steps forward required me to take two steps back. Given the home's location, we had two major obstacles that would compound the normal problems found with any new construction. First we had no hydro, and second we had no telephone.

Sticking with it, through the Learning Curve

Living off the grid is somewhat of a foreign concept still here in Canada and I was hard pressed to find a mentor who could advise me on the realities of such an endeavour. So I simply had to rely on the advice provided by the people who sold the solar products. Unfortunately, although well meaning, these people generally had no idea what they were talking about!

Getting power to the house was one of my first priorities. I had an assortment of battery powered power tools, but without a system in place to charge them they were of no use to me. There is certainly no way to build a 6,000 square foot home without using a drill or circular saw. And given the time of year I moved into this place, lighting was also a priority if I wanted to work any later than 5pm.

The Ark as it is today with solar panels on the roof and a wind turbine in the background.

I put my faith completely in the solar dealer, "Mark", who had come recommended to me. Mark was a great guy and wanted to do everything he could to help us out. He knew I didn't have much money, but he also knew I would need what was necessary to survive. In his first attempt to save me some money he sold me $15,000 in solar equipment but left out the $400 control panel. Without this control panel my system was worthless! I couldn't set anything up or regulate any of my power at all. Of course it took me days to figure this out. I didn't even know such a control panel existed and I couldn't for the life of me figure out what I was doing wrong! I talked to Mark a few times but he couldn't figure it out either. By his specs everything should be good to go! For some reason he was under the impression that the control panel was a luxury item and he thought by not including it at that time would be saving me some money.

Day after day of frustration went by before I was finally able to do my own research and figure out a piece of equipment was missing. Once I explained my suspicions to Mark, he spoke with a technical guy and sure enough, everything would be fine if we just filled that one missing link.

The problem with ignorance is that many times you don't even know when you are ignorant. I knew I didn't know very much about solar power installation, but I trusted Mark had provided me with all the tools I would need. I just assumed I was the one who was doing something wrong and every morning I would have to wake and bang my head against the wall again.

Later on it came time to install the well to bring fresh water into the house. Mark explained that a deep well pump was the best way to go, but it was essential that I install a DC (Direct Current) pump as they use far less Energy than the conventional AC (Alternating Current) pumps. Of course these specialized pumps cost more, but when you are living on a battery powered system and only have two kilowatts of power available at any given time, there really is no alternative.

So I spent the money on this specialized pump and the special wire and plumbing that accompanies it. I read the manual thoroughly and installed the pump, the pressure tank and all the associated plumbing myself. You wouldn't believe my joy the first time I saw water pouring out of my taps. For two years and two WINTERS I had been using a tarp covered outhouse as my bathroom. With the addition of indoor plumbing I would finally be able to go to the bathroom without having to brush snow off the lid before I sat down!

(This goes back to my ability to appreciate what I have. Nowadays when I get upset because my computer is acting up I can put things into perspective. Sure my computer might be running slowly, but at least now I have a warm bathroom where I can sit and think things over!)

Now that I had water running in the house my next goal was to find a method in which to warm that water. Baby wipes worked okay for general cleaning up but they really weren't much help in washing my hair or getting truly clean and fresh. Since I knew we couldn't heat water with electricity (the one thing off the grid homes can't do is purposefully produce heat. This means no portable or baseboard heaters, no clothes dryer, no toasters, electric stoves or hairdryers), I did my research and learned about propane and oil boilers that instantaneously heated water for domestic and heating purposes.

My research found that the propane boilers started around $1200 per unit and oil boilers were well over $3000 per unit. For a guy with no money and minimal remaining credit, this was a no-brainer; a propane boiler it was. A few days later a propane boiler salesman arrived at the house. I showed him the size of the place and explained the uses I had for the water. Of course, I needed hot water for showers and washing dishes, but I also intended on heating the 2,000 square foot concrete pad in the lower level.

He stated the entry level unit wouldn't be powerful enough for the task, but the $1600 unit wouldn't have any problem at all. He also said that if I were able to run plumbing from my well pump, up through my pressure tank and through the rest of the house, I wouldn't have any problem installing this boiler myself. This was perfect; I could hardly stand the anticipation of knowing my house would soon be moving to the next major stage in becoming a normal home.

A week or two later the boiler arrived at my door. It was a wall mount unit and I basically expected that I would need to hang the unit, run a cold water line in, and two hot water lines out. Was I ever surprised when I took a look at the instructions! Before this thing would work there was a veritable maze of copper pipes that needed to be installed. There were check valves, anti scald devices, a pressure tank, shunting systems and a bunch of other stuff I had never heard of before. And this all had to be done with soldered copper pipe. When I plumbed my house I simply used plastic tubing with crimped metal fittings. I was terrible at soldering!

But I'm a proponent of V.E.A.R. right? I can make this work. "If it can be done, it can be done by me!" So I started to assemble the supplies and tried to figure where to start first. Obviously with no real plumbing experience, most of the instructions may have well been written in ancient Aztec pictographs. So I called the company to get some clarification on a few things.

When they found out I wasn't a trained and licensed installer, they refused to tell me anything and advised me that if I did attempt to install this myself I would void the warranty and also possibly blow up my house! They told me that if I had any brains at all, I would call a licensed professional. I asked them if they knew of any in my area and of course they did not!

Eventually I found a plumber who said he was trained and licensed for this installation so I hired him. Of course, he couldn't give me a quote as to how much it might cost but what choice did I have? He showed up in a broken down station wagon with a mess of tools and parts in the back. I could tell by the way he was looking at the instructions that he didn't really know where to start either. But since I was no help to him, I left to work on another project of my own.

Mid afternoon he came to me to say that he had made some progress but was short a couple of parts and would return the next day to finish the job. He returned early that day and left late in the afternoon, but at least the job was progressing. Seeing the maze of pipes soldered together I knew this was a task I could not have accomplished. I honestly believe that "if it can be done, it can be done by me". I'm sure that with some education and practice I could have been successful eventually, but I simply wasn't ready to take on a task of that magnitude with my level of experience. Of course, the cost of a "professional" installation was $1200 (the original boiler salesman didn't tell me anything about this additional expense)!

A week later the propane technicians arrived to connect the propane to the boiler. I finally had hot water! The job cost me considerably more than I had anticipated and had taken longer than I had planned for, but now that I could take a hot shower it was all worth it! That afternoon I must have spent 20 minutes under the hot water. The water pressure wasn't exactly what I remember showers being, but what did I care; I was soapy, clean, and warm!

That weekend Monique arrived (she wasn't living with me prior to having heat or indoor plumbing) and I couldn't wait to show her the new developments. While she was cleaning up in the kitchen on Saturday morning, I went in for a shower. But just as soon as I got all lathered up, the water stopped!

"What the heck????"

I toweled off, threw on some clothes and went into the kitchen to see what was going on. Monique was standing in front of the sink and said that no water came out when she turned on the tap. I went downstairs to check on the pressure tank and sure enough the gauge read "0". I flipped the switch on the tank, and slowly the pressure began to rebuild. I knew I had a good well; there was plenty of water available. But it was weird that I lost pressure like that.

Back into the shower I went, shampoo in the hair, and poof, the water was gone again. "GRRRRRRRR!" Out of the shower, towel off, throw on some clothes, and into the kitchen. Monique said the same thing happened again. Checking the pressure tank I found again that it was empty, but by flicking the switch I was able to fill it again.

You are probably thinking that I was telling you this story to show you the Resolve I demonstrated with the boiler. No, not at all. This is the story of the Resolve I had to show with the water pump!

Reading the manual that came with this super expensive DC water pump I learned that at a depth of 150 feet, the pump was capable of pumping 1.6 gallons per minute. The high efficiency shower head I had installed limited water output to 2.5 gallons per minute. So what was happening was as I ran the shower I depleted the pressure tank and then started receiving water directly from the well pump itself. It struggled to provide me with 1.6 gallons per minute in the shower, but as soon as Monique turned on the tap in the kitchen, all pressure was lost and the tank turned itself off.

This was no good at all. I couldn't risk losing water pressure every time I took a shower. So I called my solar dealer, told him my problems and asked if he had any solutions. He was surprised by this information and had never considered this pump wouldn't be appropriate for my applications. He said he would talk to a technician and get back to me.

Apparently this pump had been developed for agricultural use. It was designed to pump water from a well directly into a holding tank, from the power provided by the solar panels whenever the sun was shining. The reserve in the tank was then used by the farmer for whatever his needs were. He didn't worry about water pressure; he just wanted access to water in a remote area.

Thus the solution that was suggested was for me to install some large holding tanks for water in my attic. The pump would fill these tanks at its leisure when the sun was shining, and whenever we needed water it would be delivered to us through a gravity system. Forgetting about the issues that would arise with the water tanks freezing in the winter months, Monique has long hair (which I like!), and it would take forever for her to rinse the shampoo out with a gravity fed system. This solution wouldn't work at all.

Their next solution was for me to install a big holding tank down by the boiler. I would pump water from the well with the DC pump and then run an AC jet pump from the holding tank into the pressure tank. So now instead of having one pump delivering my water, I would have two pumps and one of those pumps would be operating on alternating current!

How is that solving anything at all????

The solar guys couldn't answer that question; they just said those were the only two options I had to work with. These guys are professionals in this field right? If they didn't have a better answer then there mustn't be one.

But this is where Resolve comes in. I had a Vision, and in that Vision my wife didn't have a shaved head and I wasn't lighting fires in my attic to thaw any frozen water tanks. In my Vision, my house was "special" but it wasn't demanding and uncomfortable. I knew there had to be a solution and I knew I was the only one who would find it.

My research taught me that AC water pumps do use considerably more power than a DC pump but the biggest problem came from the Energy "hammer" that occurred when the pump started up. This hammer can be 3 to 4 times the amount of power a running motor will use. You've probably experienced this yourself. You know when your refrigerator clicks on and the lights dim for a short second. That is that Energy hammer at work.

The problem I faced was that I only had a 2 kilowatt inverter, meaning I only had 2000 watts of power available to my house at any given time (this means I can run twenty 100W light bulbs, but if I try to turn on 21, I'll overload my system and the power will shut down entirely). An AC well pump uses between 1100 and 1200 Watts of power. So my system can handle the power draw when it's running, but it will blow if it surges to 3000W at start up. Searching around the internet and various plumbing supply stores though, I was able to find a "slow start" AC deep well pump. This pump doesn't go from being "off" to full "on" in a 10th of a second (like your fridge, a vacuum cleaner, your power tools, etc), rather it slowly winds up to speed and full power, thus reducing the Energy hammer.

Essentially I had found a pump that would use four times the power of my DC water pump, but at 150 feet of well depth it would pump close to ten gallons per minute. This means that although it used four times as much power, it would only need to run for 1/5th the length of time. At the end of the day, this AC pump would use less overall power than the DC pump!

Since it was AC instead of DC and since it was capable of pumping so much more water than the original pump, I also had to replace all the wiring and tubing. When I asked the solar dealer if I could return the DC pump they said no because it had been used and it wasn't broken! To this day I still have a $1600 DC well pump collecting dust in my garage. (It is for sale though if you're interested!)

Now you're probably seeing how Resolve was so instrumental in getting me through the trials and tribulations of building the Ark, but unfortunately this story isn't over yet! Remember on the last page when I said this story of Resolve wasn't about the boiler at all, it was about the well pump?

Well I lied.

Once we had the pump issue "Resolved" (pun intended), we began a routine of showering in the morning and washing dishes at night. Well that lasted 3 days. On the fourth day only cold water emerged from the hot water tap and an ominous red LED light glowed on the boiler. I called

Mike Caldwell

the original installer, but he didn't know how to fix any of the internal mechanisms of the boiler, he only knew how to bring water in and out of it. I called the manufacturer but again they were of no help. They said I needed a licensed repairman but they didn't know of any in my area!

I have to admit, that as I type this I can feel the rage and frustration returning. Three days of phone calling later (I had to make all of these telephone calls from my neighbour's house since I still had no phone at my place) I finally found somebody capable of fixing the thing and he said he would be able to come out first thing the next week. My mornings of hot showers had come to an end.

When the repairman finally arrived, he diagnosed the boiler with a broken sensor. Of course this was a specialized part and not one he kept in his tool box. He said it would take about a week to arrive and he would return to install it when he could. So there was another week of baby wipe "baths" ahead of me!

Eventually though he did return with the part and upon installation, the hot water to our home returned. Once again, I had the pleasure of hot morning showers.

For three more days....

Broken again. Red light on. Another week for the repairman to return. But the original sensor was still in order, this time it was a different part, and of course, not one he carried with him and one he would have to order. Another week of baby wipes and warming dishwater on the woodstove, but eventually he returned, the repair was made and all was well in the world.

Until the next week when the darn thing broke again!

This was getting ridiculous. A week later when the repairman returned we discussed options. I explained I didn't have much choice, winter was approaching and if I didn't want everything in my house to freeze (AGAIN!), this thing would have to work. It not only needed to provide my domestic hot water but the hot water I would need to heat my 2,000 square foot concrete slab.

To this statement, the repairman just laughed. Did I really expect this little, wall mounted, propane boiler to heat a concrete slab of that size? I explained how the salesman said it would.

Again, more laughter, and some under the breath comments about how salespeople shouldn't be allowed to smoke crack while they are on the job.

This little wall mounted toy couldn't handle the demands of a hot shower, how was it ever going to warm two mixing trucks worth of concrete?

He was right, I guess it couldn't...

But winter was coming and I really couldn't bear the thought of spending another winter sleeping in sub freezing temperatures. As always, there was no money, and very little hope.

Again, this is where Resolve comes into play. My options were A) give up, roll over and die (which at that time seemed quite comforting), or B) continue to fight, refuse to give up and find a solution. More research lead to my discovery that oil had 33% more BTU production than a similar volume of propane and oil boilers were capable of producing considerably larger and more concentrated flames. If I seriously wanted to heat a house this size, oil was the only possibility.

There was still no way I could afford a $3000 oil boiler (although I had now already invested this much in my worthless propane unit), but showing Resolve I went back to the local oil dealer to explain to him my plight. He was very understanding and more than willing to help. He offered to sell and install the boiler with no money down and no interest. All I had to do was make reasonable monthly payments over the next three years! This was something I could work with, although I was a little bitter that he hadn't told me about that option a few months earlier!

The propane dealer agreed to take back his worthless piece of junk because he realized he'd end up paying more on the warranty repairs than he would returning my money. I was still out the $1200 for the installation though and there was nothing I could do about that.

Ultimately, patience and Resolve resulted in us finally having all the hot water and water pressure that we would ever need. In fact, we have installed 4 outdoor showers, and all 4 can be running with hot water for as long as people wish to stay in there. It really is the best system ever!

It is important to remember though that none of the V.E.A.R. components work in complete isolation and independence. I had to have a Vision of what my water system would look like, I had to have the Energy to get up day after day to fight these battles, and I had to approach each trial with a positive Attitude.

During the days when my propane unit was broken and worthless, I simply told myself that maybe I wasn't able to have a hot shower when I wanted. But at least I had cold water running, a septic system, an insulated indoor bathroom and a kerosene heater. Unlike a year earlier, I no longer had to travel to the outhouse under Arctic conditions first thing every morning. I needed to appreciate the improvements in my life instead of lamenting the luxuries I wished would arrive sooner. I also learned some lessons which would help me with further projects along the way.

The most important lesson was that when given an answer you don't like, don't take a single individual's word for it. After speaking with the solar representative about the DC well pump, I should have called an AC pump dealer to learn his perspective. Had I learned that lesson the first time around, I probably would have done more research before investing in that propane boiler.

My problem was that I had too many irons in the fire. While I was working on the well pump and hot water issues, I was still insulating sections of the house, installing vapour barriers and subfloors, finishing drywall, preparing for a wedding, building components for Corporate Synergy, soliciting clients and exercising my dogs. So as soon as I was able to pass a job onto somebody else I jumped on the opportunity. I didn't want to spend any time questioning their knowledge, abilities, motives or judgment. I just wanted to check that item off the list and move on.

I'm not sure but maybe there is another lesson in there somewhere as well...

Trials and Tribulations with Bell Canada

But without a doubt, my most glowing example of demonstrating Resolve came with my dealings with Bell Canada. As you may remember from the end of the Energy section, Bell had promised me telephone installation for $75 but when the technician arrived, the fee was raised to $45,000! Obviously I had not budgeted for this, but I was equally not surprised. In fact instead of telling everyone how excited I was to be getting a phone installed for $75, I was telling everyone there was no way I could ever be THAT lucky. So of course, the Law of Attraction brought me exactly what I expected...

I decided that I didn't need Bell. I wanted to live "off the grid" so despite them being responsible for this telephone error I decided to take action on my own and looked into every possible alternative available for connecting with the world through telephone communications.

My first plan was to simply utilize my cellular telephone, but my current provider didn't have any towers in this area. So, not having quite learned my lesson the first time around, I contacted Bell Mobility. I explained where I lived and my problems receiving service with my current provider. They reported to me that their map showed that I might be able to access a digital signal, but if that failed I was guaranteed an analogue signal. I would simply have to purchase a dual capability phone when I signed over my three YEAR PLAN to Bell Mobility.

Well that was easy! I just saved $45,000! However.... Sure enough, after canceling my old cell phone, switching over to Bell Mobility and purchasing a phone, as I drove up my driveway, my cell phone display screen read "No Service Available". What????

I called Bell Mobility (from my neighbour's house) to tell them what happened and the new operator I spoke to said that wasn't surprising given the hilly terrain I live in. I asked about the "guarantee" the previous operator gave me and I was informed that "he shouldn't have said that". Apparently there are dead spots in even the best areas of service. But luckily this operator was an "outside the box" thinker and he told me that today's cell phone's have only 0.4W of power. The older, "bag phone" cellular phones packed a whopping 3W of power. He said that if I was able to get service just down the road from my house, it was quite possible that this 3W phone would work from inside our home.

After a somewhat prolonged search I finally found somebody on eBay who was selling this retro old-style cellular telephone for $100. A few days later, and after a few more hassles with Bell, I was able to get this phone connected to my plan. Unfortunately, after all that effort this phone didn't work either. This was probably a good thing though as apparently there were medical reasons why the power of cell phones has dropped from 3W to only 0.4W of power!

The next "solution" I learned of was a cell phone amplifying device. A friend of mine is a rally car racer and he says one of his competitors swears about the enhanced reliability of these devices. I was able to find one of these amplifiers and the accompanying antenna from a company in Arizona for just under $200. A week or two later the equipment showed up in the mail, bringing with it another round of disappointment. This set up wouldn't work either.

I then decided to try a more basic antenna system in which a long antenna cable is strung above the ground perpendicular to the cell phone tower it would be accessing. But when I called Bell Mobility to learn which tower that might be and its location, they refused to tell me as that was "classified" information!

It was now obvious that cell phone service wasn't going to be my solution. My next strategy was to look into using a satellite phone. This is what we used on the helicopter and for the most part it worked just fine. Research into that revealed that the satellite telephone itself would cost $1000 and the service plan for my limited usage would be approximately $400 per month! Obviously a monthly bill like that wasn't in my budget.

I had just about run out of options, and patience, when Monique and I attended a Home and Cottage Show in Ottawa. We like these shows because they frequently have solar power dealers there with new ideas, and further ideas for rural home constructions. You wouldn't believe our joy when we learned about 2-way, high-speed, satellite internet service. This service was a $2000 initial investment and then $99/month in service fees. But these fees were for unlimited use and the salesperson explained to us the technology behind Voice Over Internet Protocol (VOIP). Apparently with high speed internet, your computer can also provide you with telephone service.

As I write this book in 2008, I have a few friends now who have DSL internet connections at home and use

VOIP as their telephone service provider. But back in 2003, this was cutting edge technology. The salesperson explained to me how he had an Ottawa client who did a lot of business in Mexico and to avoid all the long distance charges he used his VOIP account.

Finally, we had found a solution! We wouldn't need Bell and although it was a $2000 investment we hadn't budgeted for, the $99/month was a worthwhile expense as it would cover our high speed internet service as well as our local and long distance telephone charges. The relief and excitement we felt was overwhelming.

Unfortunately, the more excited you allow yourself to become, the bigger the letdown when things don't go through as planned. For my first telephone call, I called my mom. I was so excited to hear the phone ringing through my headset, and even more excited when I heard my mom pick up and say "Hello".

"Hello" I replied.

To which she said "Hello?"

"Hello" I said back, "Do you hear me?"

"Hello?" She questioned again.

"Hello, can't you hear me?"

"Is that you Mike?" she asked.

"Yeah, it's me, we finally have a phone at the house that works"

"Can you hear me?" she queried.

"Yeah I can hear you, how's the reception at your end?"

"Are you still there?" she asked.

And this was how the conversation continued until utter frustration set in and I gave up. Apparently "2-way, high-speed, satellite internet service" wasn't 2 way high speed at all. Although it was capable of 1.5 megabyte per second download speeds it was only capable of 10-40 kilobyte per second upload speeds. And then there was the additional latency period as the satellite signal traveled all the way outside the earth's atmosphere (to the satellite) only to be bounced down again to the other computer or telephone.

So although I would hear my mom speak in just 10ths of a second after she spoke, she was waiting 5 to 7 seconds to hear what I had said. Holding a conversation with this degree of sound separation was simply not possible. And there was no way I could expect potential corporate clients to negotiate with me on a system like this. But at least now we had internet service in our home and I could link to the outside world through this medium.

Since Bell Mobility refused to return any of my calls in regard to the construction of a new cell phone tower on our land I had to surrender to the fact that I would require a Bell telephone landline. There was no way I could afford $45,000 and certainly no lending institution would be foolish enough to lend me the money. But that is what Resolve is all about, continuing to fight even when it appears the battle is lost.

Here's another fitting quote from Mohamed Ali:

"Only a man who knows what it is like to be defeated can reach down to the bottom of his soul and come up with the extra ounce of power it takes to win when the match is even."

Much to my surprise, this tenaciousness paid off. Upon speaking with Bell Canada I learned about a rural telephone service initiative being offered by the CRTC (Canadian Radio-television and Telecommunications Commission). This program was designed to increase the availability of telephone service in remote regions of Quebec. Under this plan, I would be responsible for the first $1000 of installation, the CRTC would pay the next $25,000 and I would be responsible for any remaining amount.

Mike Caldwell

Although this was still hardly the best case scenario, I was now between a rock and something harder than a rock. Not having a telephone was making being self-employed nearly impossible and with no telephone here, no bank would ever provide us with a mortgage. So although I did not relish the idea of spending (borrowing) $20,000, I stood to lose considerably more if I failed to choose this option.

So I finally folded. Bell Canada had promised me telephone service for $75 and they had even admitted their mistake in doing so. They explained that their computers did not differentiate between rural and urban installations. Apparently, in the city the difference in house numbers between my home and the "next door" neighbour was small enough to allow a very simple installation. Of course, this was not the case out here in the country.

I spoke to a lawyer and he assured me I had a very strong case. But I was forewarned that this case would drag on for years and years and ultimately cost me tens of thousands of dollars. There was nothing left for me to do. I had to expand my ever growing credit card collection, borrow the money, waive my white flag and beg Bell Canada to finally install our telephone.

Now you may be thinking that this story is over. I lost, Bell won. They get their money, my situation just got tougher. But everything is now settled, I'll get my phone and life will move on...

This is not the case when you're dealing with Bell Canada; if there is a way to add insult to injury they will. In December of 2004 I paid Bell Canada their blood money and signed a contract with them that would ensure installation of my telephone line would begin before the end of May, 2005. Sure enough on May 5, 2005 all of my telephone poles were in place. Bell had lived up to their end of the bargain by beginning installation prior to the end of the month. But on September 5th, 2005, a telephone line had still not been run on these poles and I was still without telephone service!

Just to recap in December, 2004, I borrowed $20,000 at 18% interest ($300/mth) to pay Bell Canada for a telephone line. In May, the installation began, and ended. In September, or $2400 in lost interest later, I still had no telephone line! Admittedly, although I could still envision a working telephone in my house, regardless of any tricks I might have, my energy was gone and my attitude was quite poor. All I could do was show Resolve and every morning force myself to visit my neighbour and use her telephone. Every day I would call somebody different in the hopes that somebody would listen and simply install the telephone that they had promised me 3 years earlier.

Finally on September 21st, 2005 a telephone line was laid, although ON THE GROUND BESIDE THE TELEPHONE POLES and telephone communication was established at the Ark. In mid-December, the technicians returned to actually place the line on the poles. Apparently it is acceptable to leave a telephone line on the ground for years before securing it to the poles. So technically, my phone line could have been installed, in less than half a day, immediately on the day after I paid for the service.

Had things gone my way though, I would never have learned the limits to my Resolve. I was determined not to let this issue with telephone communication beat me. And day after day, week after week, month after month, and year after year, for 3 longs years I fought to bring a telephone into my house. In the end, I calculated that this telephone issue cost me in excess of $125,000. There were not only the expenses I incurred in trying to find a non-Bell Canada solution, and then the actual expenses and interest associated with installation, but not having a telephone cost me my job as a part time paramedic and

Mike Caldwell

prevented us from securing a low interest mortgage for the house.

To be honest, looking back on this now I don't know how I survived it all. I know I tried to keep a positive attitude and approach each day with a renewed energy. But every day brought with it a new struggle. I remember one challenging day when I called to speak with a certain manager at Bell Canada. Her receptionist stated that she was in a meeting and that she "would have her call (me) back".

I explained to her that she couldn't "call me back" because I didn't have a telephone!

With considerable indignation and noticeable frustration the woman said "How can she be expected to reach you then???"

It was with this comment that my head nearly exploded! "Give me a freakin' phone and I promise never to inconvenience your manager again!"

(I'm sorry, I have to change the subject and re-adjust my Energy and Attitude, my blood is beginning to boil again just by reliving that day and whole ordeal in my mind. Remember, your subconscious doesn't know the difference between reality and imagination!)

Take a Snapshot of the Moment

But seriously, how was I able to survive that ordeal and do what needed to be done day after day after day for three years straight? There were two linked processes that allowed me to get through this. The first thing you need to do in any situation is take a snapshot of that instant. Look objectively at yourself in that precise moment. In most cases, if you do that honestly and objectively you'll find you are not as bad off as you thought.

That instance when the receptionist asked how her manager was supposed to reach me was probably one of the lower points of my ordeal, so let's look at that snapshot.

I was sitting in my neighbour's house. She had become a very good friend and was very supportive of my situation. I had just eaten a good breakfast, after a good night's sleep, and I had a productive day of "Ark" construction ahead of me. My beautiful and loving wife would be home for dinner and after dinner we'd probably go for a nice walk on our own private, wooded trails with our two loyal Border Collies. Upon returning home, we'd have a quiet evening relaxing in front of the fireplace without having to worry about any annoying interruptions with a ringing telephone!

In that snapshot, my life really wasn't too bad. Certainly I had to be concerned about my mounting debt and my ability to repay it. But I needed to deal with that in a constructive manner. Getting all stressed out and worrying about the situation wasn't going to solve anything. The future was still ahead of me and anything could happen.

> The only thing any of us can control is the here and now. The future tends to look after itself.

And that was how I survived each and every day. Each day I worked toward securing a positive future, but only "worried" about the present. Throughout this entire arduous process, 10 times out of 10, when I looked at any precise snapshot of THE PRESENT, there was nothing to worry about.

There were two glowing occasions though, when although the present was in decent shape the following week or the following month was looking mighty bleak. As I mentioned, most of the funding for building the Ark was coming from increasing my 20% interest credit card debt. There was one instance in 2005 when there was no credit available to pay the interest on any of the other debts. Within a month, loans would be called in. (This was the first time I spoke with an attorney about the potential for declaring bankruptcy).

However, just prior to the arrival of "Doomsday", a captain from CFB Petawawa contacted me with interest in bringing 30 individuals from his troop for a full week of adventure training and team building to the Ark. Given all the work I had invested in preparing our onsite campground, nature trails, rappel cliffs, and conference facilities, we were able to provide the exact course the captain was looking for. This turned out to be a $28,000 contract!

I was not only able to pay the credit vultures that were circling for the kill, but I was able to purchase an All Terrain Vehicle, rope equipment, an extra refrigerator, and kitchen supplies for use with this and future clients. This contract alone brought me nearly a full year's reprieve from my debtors!

But as we moved closer and closer to the finish line of securing a mortgage, the lending institutions kept moving the line further and further back. First they said the house would need to be 90% complete before they could extend a mortgage to us. Then it was 92%, then 95%, then 98%... Finally they said the house really needed to be "100%" complete before we could qualify for a mortgage. Every percentage point they increased their demands required significantly more financial output from us. The race was most certainly on. Which would happen first? Would we "finish" the house, or would we completely exhaust our last avenue for credit?

The Ark as it looks today , 2007. The "before" picture is on page 53.

As it turned out, it was the latter. Everything in the house was completed EXCEPT for the ensuite bath in the master bedroom. In this room the subfloor had still yet to be installed and only reflective vapour barrier lined the walls. Even doing all the work myself, a bathroom of this size would easily cost in excess of $10,000.

We had already completely maxed out all of our credit and in fact in two months time, we would have no way of paying over 50% of our mandatory monthly bills. It was looking like after a long four year battle, in the end we would emerge defeated.

NEVER Accept Defeat

But what sort of motivational book would this be if that were the case! I refused to give up. In my mind the house WAS 100% complete. We had finished the living room, kitchen, dining room, study, exercise room, laundry room, two bedrooms, two walk-in closets, 3 bathrooms and a 2,000 square foot recreation room. How many homes can boast all of that? Sure, off the bedroom there is a room that is lined with vapour barrier and filled with junk, but doesn't every home need a "storage room"?

A "finished" view of the Great Room. To see the "before" picture go to page 55.

I called the bank who had previously shown the most interest in our property (in total I contacted in excess of 20 lending institutions and over the previous 4 years I had solicited each of them on 3 or 4 occasions). I simply told them my house was now complete and we believed we now met all of their conditions for mortgage approval.

Somehow through all of this both Monique and I had managed to keep our credit scores intact. We hadn't defaulted on any loans and were rarely even late in paying our minimum monthly payments. Our debt to equity ratio was abysmal however as on paper we were bringing just over $3000/mth but with minimal bill payments in excess of $5500/mth. And this didn't include the necessities like food and gas for the car! One simple mortgage payment carrying 6% interest would wipe out the dozen 20% credit card bills payments we were making every month and finally put our monthly budget back in the black!

Luckily the home inspector who came to the property to assess it for the bank had been here a year or two previous (we had so many home inspections it's easy to lose track). He couldn't believe the progress we made and the quality and attention to detail put into the home. He was certain that in the unlikely event of us defaulting on a mortgage, the bank would be able to easily sell our property for full compensation. As we walked through each room he made positive comments and made notes in his log. But all I could think about was that last room! The one room that would deny him from stating that our home was "100% complete".

Luckily that room is off the showcase room of our house, the master bedroom, and is concealed behind an opaque French door. I made no attempt to show the inspector this room and when I tried to usher him out of the bedroom he gestured toward the door and queried, "what's back there, storage?"

The master bedroom with door to ensuite bath/storage room on the left. Unfortunately a black and white photo doesn't do this room justice.

I couldn't believe it, it was like he was reading my mind! "Yep" I said, "storage." He simply nodded and left the bedroom with me.

I asked if he thought the house was 100% complete and he said that although there were a few minor details that could further improve the value of the house, it was certainly worth more than we were requesting to borrow. He was definitely going to give the bank a positive recommendation on the property.

Three days later, and four days before everything caved in on us we were approved for the mortgage. All of our credit cards and high interest loans were paid off in full. We now had one mortgage payment and one low car payment every month. We cancelled a number of our credit cards outright and reduced our credit limits on the remainder. Now when I call Monique and request she bring some milk and bread home from the store, she asks if she should pick up some orange juice and bananas as well!

Because, with our new mortgage and budget we can purchase groceries any time we want! Too many of us in North America take that for granted. But now that I've seen the other side, I'll never fail to appreciate all that I have again.

Part 5

It's Not About the

House

Throughout this book I have primarily used examples of how I used Vision, Energy, Attitude and Resolve to build my house. But there are also examples of it succeeded in advancing me in my career, assisting me in completing various endurance races, and in securing a tremendous relationship with my wife. V.E.A.R. can be used in any arena you choose and if you stick with it, it will produce results.

Money

In North America today, it seems the number one quest for people is to have MORE MONEY. Many people are of the belief that money brings happiness, and the more money one has, the happier that person will be. As I've said, I'm not a granola crunching, tree hugging, tie-dyed shirt wearing, greasy haired, communist hippy who believes money is the root of all evil and that maybe we should all just hold hands and live on the power of love in a commune somewhere.

No way, I love my possessions and cherish my vacations and fine restaurant meals. But I think that putting money above all is a dangerous endeavour. What do Kurt Cobain, Freddie Prinze, Brian Keith, and Dana Plato all have in common?

They all had a lot of money, but they also all committed suicide.

What do John Belushi, Jimi Hendrix, Jim Morrison, Judy Garland, and Elvis Presley all have in common?

They too had a ton of money. Apparently the money didn't make them happy enough and they all turned to drugs. All of them died of drug overdoses.

Obviously then, money isn't the answer to every question. The above examples of death are extreme cases but how many times has the pursuit of money destroyed a relationship or broken apart a family?

Mike Caldwell

I have identified that for the most part, it's not money I want, but what money can buy. This is an important differentiation. What good is being a millionaire if you're locked up in jail? Would having a million dollars be the answer to all of your dreams if you were a bed ridden quadriplegic? How much enjoyment would you get from a big pile of money if you had no friends or loved ones to share it with?

A big pile of money is actually of little use if you have nothing to spend it on. So instead of focusing on the money, focus on what it is you think it will buy. In my case, when I returned to Canada from Colorado my dream was to own a home, a new car and a cottage on a lake. This is what I focused on and within a year I had secured a decent paying job on the air ambulance which provided me with a salary that would allow me to afford all of the above.

But once those goals had been accomplished, I had a new dream of actually living in the woods in a large home with complete privacy. I probably could have achieved that dream by securing a better, higher paying job. But the downside to that would be that I would probably spend so much of my time working, I wouldn't have any time to enjoy the house!

So instead, the universe found a way to give me that home and ensure that I would have all the time in the world to enjoy it. Looking back, there were definitely a few days when I would have preferred to simply have a high paying job and lots of money. I could then have simply purchased a finished home similar to this one and would never have had to deal with all the stress and uncertainty that I experienced during those four years of construction. Those four years were definitely tough, but now that they have passed I can sit here at my desk, writing this book while I look out the window at the deer making their way through the snow in the woods. Had I gone the high salary route, right now I would be away at work stressing about some project and dreaming of either 7pm or the weekend when I could finally return home and enjoy the place.

Except for those two years working on the air ambulance, I have never really made very much money. Yet I have traveled Europe, North, South, and Central America. I have downhill skied at Whistler, Vail and Aspen. I have dined in the finest restaurants, attended national level sporting events and rock concerts, and have witnessed a ballet at the Paris Opera House. I now live in a 6,000 square foot, off-the-grid home on 164 acres of rolling hardwood forest in the Gatineau Hills. At 39 years old, I have already lived a very rich and fulfilling life.

I have done so, not by focusing on and pursuing money (although that is one option), but rather by focusing in on a high "quality" of life. I have friends who live in New York City. They probably both earn 5 or 6 times what I earn in a year. They both work 12 hour weekdays as well as Saturdays. They see very little of one another or have time to take advantage of all that NYC has to offer. But every year, they take a glorious two week vacation. No expense is spared and they absolutely have the time of their lives.

The difference between my wealthy friends and me is that they live in euphoria for two weeks every year, and I exist that way every single day of my life! If you could choose right now between tons of money combined with two weeks of annual happiness, or an empty bank account and endless joy day after day, what would your choice be?

My advice here is simply to be careful for what you wish for. If you apply V.E.A.R. your "wish" will be granted but that doesn't mean your happiness will be.

Here is a fun little game that will help you decide whether it is money or something else in life that you truly covet. The game starts in your imagination with Ed McMahon knocking on your door. You open the door and there he is holding a cheque for a million dollars. Of course the first thing you're going to do is jump up and down and scream your fool head off. But then what?

Ed gives you your cheque, you pose for a photo opportunity and he leaves. The next morning you go to the bank and deposit your cheque. You look at your bank statement and it now reads: $1,000,012.47. If "money" is your true goal in life, your imagination should now be able to hold this picture in your mind forever.

I'm betting however, that you won't be able to focus on that bank statement for very long. You're a millionaire now, what are you going to do? Is your first thought to: buy a new house, a new car, take a vacation? Let your mind go, let your daydreams take you where they may.

This isn't a one time experiment. You'll need to do this exercise day after day for at least a couple of weeks. Initially, your day dreams will be all over the map. You'll be buying expensive clothes and jewelry, you'll jet off to the south of France for dinner, you'll pay off your parent's mortgage. But over time, your day dreams will start to revisit the same thing more and more and these dreams will become more comprehensive. Instead of just buying a new house, you'll know what neighbourhood it's in, you'll see it decorated; you may even know what colour the roof shingles are.

Now we're getting there. Now we're getting to the heart of what it is you really want. This is what you would spend your money on if money weren't an issue. But since we're living life in the real world and not in our day dreams, money IS an issue. So now you need to start looking at options. Now that you know what you want, you need to start thinking outside the box about how you are going to get it.

If you were to purchase this thing now, how much would it cost?

With your current savings and salary, can you afford it?

If the answer is "yes", then what are you waiting for? Seriously, if you can afford it but haven't bought it yet, maybe it's not something you truly want in the first place. Maybe this item is destined to simply stay in your daydreams. This is an issue you need to resolve on your own before you move forward.

If the answer is "no, you can't afford it now", is this something you will be able to afford in the future with your current level of earning?

If the answer to this question is "yes", then now is the time to start working on your budget. How much money can you afford to set aside every week? Is this item more important to you than: Eating out for lunch every day? Professional highlights in your hair every month? Friday night beers with the boys every week? Are you willing to sacrifice some smaller things now, for the bigger thing down the road?

I'm a big fan of writing things down and checklists. For a few days or even a week, write down where you are currently spending your money. Once that is in place, you can objectively see where you can cut some of the fat. Then write that down. You can save: $2/day on your morning coffee (bring a thermos instead – a net gain of $8/week or $32/mth or $416/yr!), decrease your satellite TV subscription from the $63/mth package to the $37/mth package, bike to work instead of driving (saves you gas $$ and parking)... Once you write everything down, you'll be surprised to learn all the areas in which you can save. But keep in mind, this won't be easy. You'll definitely have to use V.E.A.R. to be truly successful.

Once you have done all of the math and figured out that you'll be saving $148/mth, you now need to actually SAVE that money. Don't give yourself an option. Open up a new savings account (preferably one of those online accounts that don't charge any service fees), and have $74 automatically deducted from every paycheck and deposited into that account.

Now you have to ask yourself "is $148/mth enough"?

If it is and you figure that in 9 months you'll be able to afford that thing you've always wanted, then GREAT, your problems are solved. But if it's not, and you've figured it's going to take you 2,000 months (166 years) to save up enough money for that $300,000 home, then you need to look at other options. A simple savings plan with your current level of income is not going to cut it.

First you need to look at your current profession. What are you doing now? How much are you making? How much would you need to earn to afford that $300,000 house? What does the highest paid person in your field earn?

If you are in a job earning $40,000/yr but you figure you need $70,000/yr to afford that house, what options do you have to fill that gap? Are you in a profession where promotions are available and attainable? What would you need to do to secure that next promotion or raise? Maybe you need to work longer hours... Maybe you need to take some night school classes and earn some further certifications. But are there even people within your company earning $70,000/yr? If so, what do they have that you don't?

If it can be done, it can be done by YOU!

But if the only person in your company is who is earning that sort of money is the son of the owner, then maybe it's time to look at other options.

Keep in mind, at the start of the book I promised you that V.E.A.R. works. I never promised you that it would be easy. If you are looking for "easy" please be sure to buy my next book "How to rob a bank and not get caught"!

V.E.A.R. requires Vision. Can you actually see yourself living in that $300,000 home? If so, is that picture in high definition with surround sound? What are you doing in that house? Are you just sitting there on the kitchen floor? When you come in the door after a long day of work, what are you wearing? Are you still wearing your McDonalds uniform? Or are you wearing a suit and tie?

When you sit down for dinner are you sitting there alone or do you have somebody to dine with? If you are sharing the table, what are they wearing? Is she wearing a K-Mart cashier's apron, or is she in the latest business power suit? Maybe you are in your McDonald's uniform and maybe she's in the power suit... That could be your solution there!

Why earn the money if you can marry it????

I'm kidding a bit here, but my point holds true:

> There is always more than one road leading to the same destination.

You don't necessarily have to earn $70,000/yr on your own, you just need to create a combined family income of that much.

You don't need to stay in the same job you're in now, you could work for advancement, or you could change careers entirely.

There may be other options for earning more money. You could get a part time job working weekends. Perhaps after a year or two you'll have a down payment that is large enough that you can reduce your monthly mortgages to a level your current salary can handle.

When I was working as a paramedic in Hamilton, I remember a couple of my coworkers going over to Saudi Arabia to work on the ambulances there for three month contracts. All of their expenses were paid and they would return with a nice little nest egg (and some interesting stories on the side). Similarly I know of construction workers who go down to work in areas following a disaster. They work 12 hour days, day after day without a break, but they all return home to their old jobs with a sizeable down payment for their new home.

Or you can do what I did and forget about buying a $300,000 home entirely. Simply quit your job, liquidate all off your assets, find a cheap piece of land, and build it yourself!

Regardless of the path you choose, the route to success is there. If your Vision is clear enough, you attack the challenge with Energy and a positive Attitude, and you refuse to quit and show Resolve, you will succeed. It's the only option.

Fitness

Over the past four years I have raced in two iron distance triathlons, two marathons, two Keskinada Ski Loppets, as well as a handful of adventure racers and shorter distance triathlons. Reading this book you have learned that over this time period my main priorities were the completion of my home and the settling of our finances.

"When then, did I have time to train?" you might ask.

Well the answer is; I really didn't have much time to train at all. Generally through the summer I tried to get out once or twice a week running on the trails with my dogs. But that was more for them than it was for me. And if I could, I'd like to get in one long bicycle ride on the weekends. In the winter months, it was the same thing except instead of running I would snowshoe, and on the weekend I'd try and work in a cross country ski.

Most people would never even attempt an Ironman or a marathon with this minimal commitment to training. Most of these people don't believe completing these events to be even possible without 15 to 20 hours of specific training per week! I guess I have a few things going for me though:

1) I don't lead a sedentary lifestyle. During those years of "Ark construction" I was hauling lumber and drywall up and down stairs, I was climbing ladders, I was up and down from my knees to my feet countless times a day... Since we heated the house with wood I was cutting trees, hauling logs and swinging an axe for hours at a time... I was using our trails for races and training so I was hiking and raking them, clearing deadfall... And then through the winter there was all the energy my body used just trying to stay warm! So although I didn't have time for much proper "training", I was always on the move and exercising my heart and muscles.

2) Knowing that I hadn't put much time into training, I never entered any event with unrealistic goals or expectations. My main objectives for each race were to push myself to the best of my ability and have fun and enjoy the day. I rarely put the strain on myself for having to beat another competitor (okay there was the one "Giles is GOING DOWN!" ordeal) or to set a "personal best".

Despite these "limiting" factors though, I actually ended up performing relatively well. I just reviewed the last 10 races that I have competed in and learned that on average I have finished in the top 42% of the race field! I didn't include my two Keskinada results in that calculation as in those events I finished in the top 90 and 95% of the fields! Yikes, I am NOT a good skier at all!

So if I wasn't focused on training and I didn't take the events all that seriously, what then made my race success possible? (I had one first place finish in the Somersault Kayak Triathlon and a fifth place finish in a half iron distance Aquabike).

V.E.A.R. of course!

Mike Caldwell

I entered every race with a Vision of how that race would unfold. I always envisioned myself, working hard and "feeling the burn" but at the same time relishing in the joy of simply being alive and able to take part in an event such as this.

I would start every race with my Energy at its maximum level. There is so much Energy in the corral at the start of a race; I would simply stand in the middle of all the racers, I would clear and relax my mind and drink all that Energy in. On the course, I would tap into my own personal Energy reserves as much as possible, and when it was available I would take advantage of the Energy being provided to me by the spectators and other competitors.

On the course I would never fail to appreciate where I was or what I was doing. Racing an Ironman or a marathon or even an 8k run is something special. Racing reminds me that I am healthy and alive. With that at the forefront of my mind, it's not very difficult to maintain a positive Attitude.

Unfortunately not many racers share this view with me and tend to look at me as though I'm some sort of freak when I greet them and encourage them on with a big smile on my face. They simply can't understand why I'm not suffering like they are, and I can't understand why that, given a choice, they have chosen to suffer!

Of course, I'm not perfect and the previous few paragraphs have described the way I would like every race to unfold. Most race days are great for me but some days the weather may not cooperate. Other days (or maybe the same day!), I may just not be able to access my energy stores as I am used to. There have been a couple of races where my knee starts giving me pain or my bike keeps mysteriously skipping gears.

It is on days like this where I have to resort to my Resolve. I can see the Vision, I know the Energy is there, and I have no reason not to have a positive Attitude, but there is a difference between intellectually "knowing" something and feeling and living it in your core. This is when Resolve kicks in. You have to believe things will improve and keep motivating yourself until all the pieces finally come together. The pieces are always available, but there are times when assembly is a little tougher than others.

V.E.A.R. need not be solely utilized during competitive events. Its application is just as useful in training for races or in simply exercising for personal health and fitness. Inertia is a terribly powerful force and again, if you are moving in the right direction then it serves as a good thing, but if you are stationary or moving backwards it can be very bad. V.E.A.R. is the tool used to overcome inertia when necessary.

Unless you are a professional athlete and your livelihood is dependent upon your results, I don't recommend placing too much emphasis on them. I'm not saying you should ignore them entirely, but don't use your most recent 10k road run time to judge your overall person. Your main goal should always be to do the best you can on that given day. A secondary goal may be to set a new personal best for yourself, but if you fail to do so, always look to your primary goal for validation of your experience.

Last month I did a telephone interview with triathlon legend Mark Allen. He and Dave Scott were two of my biggest heroes growing up. Mark and I spoke about the 1987 Hawaii Ironman World Championship Race. Dave Scott had won this event five times already and Mark Allen had failed to post a victory on this course. 1987 was the year Mark planned on changing all of that.

As always, it was extremely hot on the island of Kona, but Mark paid no attention to the heat, his sole focus was on the finish. He set a blistering pace on the bike, leaving Dave Scott in the dust. But with Mark's overwhelming focus on speed, he failed to listen to his body and failed to hydrate and nourish it to the level it required.

Part way through the run, Mark's body started to break down. Allen had pushed it too hard and he was in too deep to recover on the course. With only two miles to go, Mark experienced a complete physical melt down. It was all he could do to stay upright and finish the race. In the end, Dave Scott claimed his 6th victory and Mark finished in 5th place overall.

Prior to this race, Mark Allen was in a mental conflict with himself. He admitted to me that he was generally not a very happy person. He believed happiness would not be his until he won in Hawaii. But in 1987 he had an epiphany, there was a chance he would never win this event. And if that was indeed the case, then he would never be happy.

With the help of a shaman, Mark was able to find internal peace. He no longer judged himself based on his results, rather he judged himself on his performance.

Mark had entered the race in 1987 with the intent of winning. When his legs buckled and racers began to pass him, that dream was over. He could barely walk, there was no way he could win. That victory had been snatched from him after years of dedication and focus.

Had I been in the condition Mark was in and had my dream just vanished before my eyes, I think I would be very tempted to quit then and there and seek medical attention. I asked Mark what he was thinking and why he refused to quit under such bleak circumstances.

Mark told me that at that moment his focus shifted from the end result to his own personal drive. He was committed to giving 100% to that race. Two miles from the finish, his body had broken down to the point that it was only physically capable of performing to 20% of its usual capacity. But Mark was determined to give 100% of that 20% that was remaining.

> Pain is temporary, quitting is forever –
> Lance Armstrong

In our interview, Mark said "Some people believe that if they have a great race, then they'll be happy about their life. I used to be that way, but the opposite is true. When I was trying to gain a result, it actually strangled me from attaining the finish I was after. In 1989, I went into the race just happy to be there and that was the first year I won."

But it wasn't his last. Mark Allen went on to tie Dave Scott's record of six Ironman World Championship victories. The victories came after he stopped judging himself based solely on his race performance. If Mark Allen can race with a philosophy of simply being there to enjoy the experience, what is stopping you from racing with the same outlook?

This philosophy isn't restricted to racing either. It can be applied to specific training workouts or even to basic exercise. Too many people have a preconceived notion in their head as to how a particular training exercise should unfold.

Let's say for example, that you are training for a 10k race or to simply lose some excess pounds. On this given day, you are set to go out and run 6km. Perhaps you've been stressed at work or with your family and on this day you simply can't get your mind focused on the workout. You try and hold that Vision of crossing the 10k finish line, or fitting into that old pair of jeans, but every time you conjure up that Vision, your mind introduces your boss into the picture!

You try and draw energy from that infinite life source of yours but it's not emerging. You can't focus, you have no Energy, you don't want to be running, but you know you have to. You decide that when all else fails, you can always control your Resolve and you stick it out. You are scheduled to run 6km, and that is precisely what you are going to do! But as soon as you come to that first hill, you know there is no way you'll be able to run it and so you walk. You've run this hill before so you know you can do it, but it's just not in you today. When you do start running again, your stride is jerky and you can't find your rhythm. Eventually you make it home, but it took you 10 minutes longer than it should have.

You hate running and you nearly hate yourself! What a ridiculous waste of time. You're never going to finish that 10k and you may as well throw out those old jeans right now! What were you thinking in ever attempting something like this in the first place?

Do you see the negative spiral all of us have slipped into in one arena or at one time or another? You need to step back and look at things more objectively. What is the goal you are shooting for?

You want to finish a 10k running race?

Is that race today?

No.

Is it tomorrow?

No.

Are you having a bad day today?

Yes.

Does one bad day make you a bad person?

No.

Is running TODAY absolutely critical to the success of your overall goal?

No.

If you skipped today's run altogether, would that make you a bad person?

Of course not!

V.E.A.R. is an awesome tool, but it's not 100% effective. There are some days that are simply out of synch, and there is nothing you can do to get back on track. This is a normal part of life. Accept that and don't judge yourself for it. Give yourself a break and instead of trying to force an issue, take a deep breath and relax. Allow yourself some time to recharge your batteries. V.E.A.R. will still be there tomorrow, as will your goal of completing that 10k race.

You need to keep your focus on the big picture. In this example of completing a 10k race, you may have 100 days leading up to the culmination of your goal. So what if you have an off day! Or 5 off days, or even 10!. Even if you have 10 bad days, you're still batting 90%, and my bet is that 90% will allow you to reach your goal.

What if you're trying to lose 10 pounds? Now you have even more breathing room to play with. This goal is more about the journey than the destination. Losing 10 pounds is more about living a healthy lifestyle than it is losing the weight. Some people can stop putting sugar in their coffee and lose 5 pounds overnight. Others may cut all fat and simple sugars from the diet, start exercising 3 times a week, and it will still take them a month to lose 2 pounds. You can't judge yourself on the destination, your focus needs to be on the journey.

I personally started "training" a lot more as I made my way through writing this book. The term "training" has always held negative connotations for me. I don't know why and there is no rational reason behind it. I've just never taken my athletic pursuits very seriously and thus felt silly scheduling myself for a training session. Racing isn't a priority in my life and it's not something that is very important to me. So why should I go out and "train" for something I don't overly care about and for something I am doomed not to succeed in.

While writing this book however, I realized that I was placing judgment on something that shouldn't have been judged. I may not like training, but I enjoy running with my dogs. So my dogs (and me) were missing out on our runs simply because I was caught up on the description I was giving the task. I didn't run because I didn't want to feel foolish training for something I was never going to do well in.

I have since removed this label and for the past few weeks have been running every other day. I missed a couple of days earlier this week because it was abnormally cold and windy. But that is fine with me. My goal isn't to log 50km a week on the road, nor is it to run a sub 3:40 marathon. My goal now is to get out and enjoy myself running with my dogs as many days as I can. If I ran when it was -30C outside, I wouldn't have been achieving my goal because I wouldn't be enjoying myself.

With an attitude like this, how many kilometers a week do you think I'll end up running? Right now I'm running a little more than 30km per week on average. But I'm only running 10k at a time. Next week I plan on bumping my short runs up to 12km. I have a new GPS "Training" watch now, and part of the fun for me is racing against the fastest pace I've previously posted.

I know that sounds an awful lot like training, but I'm not defining it that way. It really is just something I'm having fun doing. But if I keep increasing my mileage, and racing my own fastest posted time, what do you think is probably going to happen to my marathon time?

My personal best marathon time to date is 3 hours and 54 minutes and I did that without running a step in the two months preceding the event! I'm not going to set any time goals for myself, because I don't need any additional pressure in my life right now. I will however probably spontaneously enter a marathon sometime this summer or fall, just to see what rewards enjoying the journey will bring me.

Once again, it all comes down to perspective. For most of us, it is hard to maintain doing something we "have to" do. It's always a lot easier to continue doing that which we "want to" do. The best tool for making the transition from "have to" to "want to" is by removing the judgment. Don't judge your actions based on expected or anticipated results. Rather simply enjoy and appreciate the journey for what it is.

Relationships

It's ironic that I've left this subject to the end of my book. It's ironic because I am displaying the precise behaviour this chapter is going to warn you about!

What many of us fail to realize is that our relationships are THE most important things in our lives. Think about all the other stuff that is important to you: money, a nice house, a nice car, exotic vacations, fine dining, movies, sporting events, walks in the woods... Now imagine having ALL of those things to excess, but you are all alone...

How glorious is that home if you only ever rattle around in it by yourself? How fun is paragliding in Mexico if you are on that vacation alone? How "fine" is dining at the restaurant of a world famous chef if you are seated at a table for one?

None of that other stuff really matters if you are walking through this world on your own. Now when I refer to relationships, most people probably think I'm referring to husband and wife, or boyfriend and girlfriend, or boyfriend and boyfriend, whatever! But no, there are plenty of single people in the world who have very fulfilling lives. Instead of that "special someone", these happy single folks usually have a decent network of friends they can rely on.

For the purpose of this book though, I'm going to focus on the application of V.E.A.R. toward that one special relationship. Hopefully most of you agree that "things" in life lose their appeal if they can't be shared. Isn't it funny then how much time many of us spend on the pursuit of things at the expense of maintaining our relationships?

You can use V.E.A.R. in a relationship the same way you use it to further your career, earn more money, improve your physical fitness or build a house! The process is the same and the amount of work is similar too. The first step is to envision that perfect relationship. The pitfalls in this Vision are similar to the pitfalls found with the pursuit of money. It's not the money you want, it's the stuff money can buy.

Similarly, don't try to envision that perfect man or woman (we'll use "man" from here on out, just to save a few letters on the page), rather envision the perfect relationship. Because, I hate to break it to you, but no one of us out there is "perfect", and once you realize that you'll understand that you'll never find the "perfect" guy.

But a perfect relationship is possible, because that is the interaction between two people. And with two people, compromise can create a middle ground where everyone wins. So in your Vision, don't imagine a tall, dark, handsome stranger walking into your life. Rather envision a picture with the two of you together, talking, laughing and playing. Isn't that what you really want? Someone to laugh with and play with, someone you can trust and who will trust you, and someone you can love and will love you.

That should be your goal as that is what will ultimately make you happy. If instead you spend all of your time pining away for a Brad Pitt look-alike, that is eventually what you'll probably find. But if your Vision didn't equally emphasize the qualities of humour, compassion, and caring, then be prepared for the consequences. A lasting, positive relationship can't be built on the packaging; it needs to be based on the contents.

So when forming your Vision, give some serious thought and consideration to the qualities you are searching for in that special someone. Are you looking for someone who is: kind, outgoing, funny, reliable, intelligent, responsible, loving, caring, attentive, good looking? What qualities are most important to you and which ones will ultimately make you happy?

Use these characteristics to build a clear, concise Vision in your mind. If looks aren't all that important to you, then try not to put a face on your mystery man. If you do that, it's the face you'll be keeping an eye out for and not the true qualities that will make you happy.

Finding the guy is only the first step in the process and your Vision will be your biggest asset here. But once he's found, then it's time to apply the Energy, Attitude and Resolve. Think for a minute about the people you are drawn to; I don't mean only romantically. I mean the people who you like to have in your company. Why is it that you like to be around these people?

Most often it is because these people have a positive Attitude and a high level of Energy that uplifts you. Since we all like to be around people we like, why don't you become one of those people! Who is a man likely to be more attracted to, the woman moping quietly on the sidelines, or the woman in the heart of the action? People of action are always positive and possess high energy. This behaviour will not only draw somebody to you, but it will keep them interested once a relationship has formed. Energy cannot be destroyed, it can only move from one form to another. This makes it infectious! If you want to be with someone who is positive and upbeat, you have to start that way yourself. Like attracts like and you will attract the mirror to yourself.

Most relationships require effort. They can easily be compared to making money. Let's say you go to an interview and get hired for that $100k a year job. But on Monday, you don't show up for work. Nor do you arrive on Tuesday, Wednesday, Thursday... How many paychecks do you think you'll be receiving? Probably not very many.

It's the same in a relationship. You may find and land your soul-mate, but if you don't "show up" to the relationship, it will fail. You need to continue to pump Energy into yourself, your partner and the relationship. No relationship is perfect, but instead of focusing on the negative, be sure to appreciate the positive.

I, like most guys, never clean the bathroom in our house. I also fail to cook dinner as often as I should. If Monique wanted she could focus on these (and my other) faults and bring the entire relationship down. But instead, she focuses on the beautiful bathroom I built for her, the support I give to her, and to the love I attempt to display for her in so many other ways.

Appreciate what you have and not what you're missing. If Monique and I weren't together she would be cleaning the bathroom anyways and cooking ALL of her dinners. Plus she wouldn't have a bathroom built for her nor anyone to support and love her. (I know if she wasn't with me, she'd be with somebody else, but it's doubtful that guy would be cleaning the bathroom either!)

In a good relationship, if you have chosen the right Vision and extended the right Energy and Attitude, you should rarely need Resolve. But should times grow tough, remember the reasons the two of you came together and know things will get better. If you look at your situation objectively you'll probably find things are not as bad as they seem. Continue to appreciate all that is good and show a positive attitude and before you know it, it won't be like you are showing Resolve at all. You're simply enjoying life.

Step by Step

V.E.A.R.

Mike Caldwell

If you're anything like me you love to have things spelled out clearly for you. So I've done my best to "package" V.E.A.R. in a step by step process. You'll probably need to customize it a bit to suit your own situations and needs, and you'll probably want to add a little bit of your own mojo, but this outline should definitely get you started!

Step 1: Determine Your Vision

Take some time, really think about and answer the following questions:

1. How would you rate your life out of 10 (10 being the absolute best) in the following areas?

_____ Money

_____ Career

_____ Relationship

_____ Family and Friends

_____ "Special" relationship

_____ Health and Fitness

_____ (   ) insert your own here

2. Given these scores, which 2 or 3 arenas (no more) are you most willing to improve to make the biggest difference in your life?

_____

_____

_____

3. What are the three things you most love (Appreciate) about your life?

_____

_____

_____

4. What three things are you currently "tolerating" the most right now?

_____

_____

_____

5. While looking at all of your answers above, what ONE thing would most improve your life right now?

_____

Now use this answer to create a Vision of your life or situation six months or a year from now. Take your time with this to ensure all of your senses are enrolled in the process. Can you see it? Hear it? Feel it? Smell it? Taste it? Where are your emotions? Who are you with?

Now you need to see how long you can hold this Vision for. Is it fleeting or does it continue to evolve? Does it stir a passion within you when you go there?

If you can't hold the Vision or if it doesn't elicit any passion, you need to review your answers above, correct them where necessary and start the process again. Don't move on until your Vision excites you and holds your concentration.

The next step is to conjure up that Vision again tomorrow and the day after that. If day by day your Vision grows more intense then you have chosen the right one. But if your Vision begins to dwindle and bore you, then you need to start from the beginning again.

Please don't rush this step. This is the foundation for where you'll be placing all your Energy, Attitude and Resolve. You don't want any of these to be misdirected.

Step 2: Finding the Energy

Where is the Energy for realizing this Vision going to come from? This isn't a rhetorical question? I'm asking you!

Where is this Energy going to come from? (Write it down)

Obviously you have your internal life Energy you can draw from. Accessing this Energy takes practice though. If everyone could benefit from this anytime we wanted and as often as we wanted, we'd all be running across the Sahara with Ray! So don't place any undo stress on yourself. Start slow and build day by day. The more you work on it, the more proficient you will become.

Friends, family members and loved ones are also a tremendous source of Energy. Who can you enroll to help you with this process? Keep in mind they need to believe in you and already possess positive Energy and Attitude themselves. You don't want to rely on an overly conservative, pessimistic person who doesn't believe in anyone pursuing their dreams! You need someone who will skip across a parking lot with you if that is what it will take to increase your Energy level. Make sure their names are written there right now.

Now go and speak with these people. Tell them what you want to do and how you are going to do it. Tell them all you need from them is their Energy and support and ask them if they are willing to accept that role?

_____

_____

_____

Step 3: Securing the Right Attitude

If you have just completed steps 1 and 2, you are probably fairly excited and positive right now. But how are you going to maintain these feelings in the weeks, months, or years ahead?

Right now, write down the reasons why you are feeling the way you are. What are you looking forward to? How is your life going to be better? Why are you so confident you will succeed? Write down as much and as many reasons as you can. If you're going to need more room to write, go get yourself another sheet of paper right now.

Mike Caldwell

Admittedly, you haven't actually physically started on obtaining your goal yet. You're still in the mental and planning stages. You may not have secured that goal yet, but I bet you have a number of positive things going on in your life right now. What people or things do you have in your life which you truly Appreciate? Write those answers down here:

Are you sure that is all you can come up with? Forget who you are for a minute and imagine you are a small orphan living in poverty with no access to food, medication, education, or shelter. What aspects of the life you are currently living would be envied by an individual in that situation? You don't have to live in a half million dollar home to appreciate having a roof over your head and indoor plumbing! Write down more stuff right now.

Step 4: What's your motivation?

Right now, why are you determined to stick with this? What's in it for you? How is your life going to be better? What will you no longer have to tolerate? What will success allow you to enjoy? It is the answers to these questions that are going to help you with your Resolve. Write those answers down here.

Step 5: In Your Face!

In order for this V.E.A.R. process to work, it needs to be lurking in your subconscious 24 hours a day. Constant mental reminders will not only keep your Energy and Attitude high, but it will also enlist the powers of "the Secret". This Vision is the last thing you should see in your mind before you fall asleep and the first thing you should see upon wakening.

I'd recommend creating some physical reminders to help you stay on track and focused. We all may have different ways of doing this. I am personally a visual person who is fond of checklists. So what I would do is prepare an 8.5x11 "poster" of the previous four steps. I would have the four "Step" headings with bullets underneath to remind me of my Vision, where I'll find my Energy, what I have to Appreciate, and why my Resolve will ultimately improve my life.

You may not need to be so literal. Instead, if it's a new car or an improved body you want, you may just need a photograph of that car or of a set of "6 pack" abs! But regardless of what type of poster or picture you use, you should have at least three copies: one in your office, one by your bed, and one on the fridge. You may also want additional copies in the bathroom, by the sofa, in the car...

Further, if you've decided you're not going to go through this alone and you have somebody supporting you through this process, enlist their aid even further. Set it up that every Monday night at 7pm the two of you will have a half an hour telephone call or "meeting" at the coffee shop. Your friend can be there to help you: With accountability; are you meeting your pre-goals? With solutions; why aren't you meeting your pre-goals? Or simply with an Energy boost! Daydream together! Talk about what your life is going to be like: in your new home, with your new spouse, in your new car, with your new fitness... Don't be afraid to dream. The sky is the limit. In fact, shoot for the stars and settle for the sky!

V.E.A.R. is an incredibly powerful tool. It has worked for me for longer than I even knew that it was VE.A.R. that I was using. And since I have become conscious of the four elements of V.E.A.R., I have yet to not meet with success in any endeavour I have truly pursued.

Like I said at the very start of this book, you won't find any small print at the bottom of any of these pages. RESULTS ARE TYPICAL. I'm not being humble, you've now read about my missteps and trials and tribulations. And you know I don't wake up every morning bouncing around like Richard Simmons. There really is nothing special about me at all. The only thing that makes me different than many people is that for 90% (or greater) of each and every day, I am genuinely happy with my life.

And for me, that is awesome. Because more than wanting a nice home, a productive career, a loving relationship, I want to be happy. It just so happens that the items on that list are what makes me happy! But aside from being so tall, dam good looking (and humble), the only other thing that sets me apart from anybody else is my application of V.E.A.R.

Trust me, if it works for me, there is no doubt it will work for you!

Have fun and enjoy.

Post Script:

The Ark Today

The Ark today is now pretty much what I dreamed it would be. There's still work to be done: the back deck needs to be constructed, the master bedroom propane fireplace needs to be installed, the garage space can be improved, the ensuite bathroom still needs EVERYTHING... But we can now live here in total comfort. We couldn't ask for anything more in our dream home. In fact, the projects still outstanding are part of what makes this place so great. I love having a Vision, and using all the components of V.E.A.R. to make things a reality. That's one of the reasons I love most about living here, there'll always be a new addition and a new dream to pursue.

Corporate Team Building at the Ark

More so than just a home, the Ark is also developing nicely on the business side of things. We've now hosted close to 30 corporate clients here for team building and/or leadership development. The programs we offer here are unique in that they truly capture the essence of work based problems within an outdoor experiential environment. This uniqueness is continued and further emphasized with this location. This is not a 5 Star resort or upscale hotel meeting room. The Ark is raw, it is real.

Being off the grid and surrounded by nature brings participants back to the basics. And 9 times out of 10, that is precisely what they are looking for. Systems and people tend to make life far more complicated than they need to be. Teams are able to take a collective deep breath here and re-focus on what's important. With the perfect mix of action and reflection, teams always leave here much stronger and more dedicated than when they arrived. There is a powerful future for the development of teams and leaders here at the Ark.

A Team works in unison to succeed in the "Plank Walk of Doom"!

For more information on team building, leadership and the programs available at the Ark, please visit our websites: www.team-building-leadership.com and www.synergyark.com.

Weddings at the Ark

One of the biggest pushes to get a job done came during the weeks immediately preceding our wedding. It was our dream to get married at the Ark, but as you may have guessed, there was a lot of work to be done, and none of it came without a few misadventures. For example, the $1200 worth of drywall that I ordered for the reception hall was delivered during a rainstorm. It wasn't properly covered during transport and arrived here soaking wet. It took a full week to dry it all out, and once dry, many of the sheets became curved.

Weddings at the Ark couldn't be more perfect.

On our wedding day, an unprofessional shuttle driver resulted in the bride arriving an hour late. There were a few rain showers during the ceremony, and as a result of our solar panels being stolen and a problem with the generator, I had a misadventure ingesting gasoline (these stories I'll save for my next book). But despite all of this, the wedding went off "without a hitch". I am completely serious when I say every person in attendance said that was the best wedding they had ever been to. And so, a few years later, after I had been ordained as a clergy for the All Season's Church, we decided to add weddings and receptions to our revenue stream.

Here is what the Ark looked like 48 hours before our ceremony (I'm installing lights in the center, Lance is staining the trim), and what it looks like today!

Going into our second year, we have now hosted three weddings here at the Ark. We currently have 6 ceremonies booked for the summer of 2008. For couples looking for an economical, outdoor, natural setting, there really is no better place than the Ark. It's just so peaceful and relaxed here, couples feel like they are wedding in their own home.

For more photos and information on wedding ceremonies and receptions at the Ark please visit: www.synergyark.com.

Races

On average it takes 5 years for a business to show a profit. As you've now read, I needed money throughout the process of building the Ark. My business plan initially involved team building using outdoor experiential education. This is primarily a seasonal business (spring, summer, and fall). In fact, just last month (February, 2008) was the first time I hosted a team (from the Office of the Auditor General) here for a winter session.

In order to bring in some money during the long Canadian winters, I established the only winter snowshoe race series in eastern Canada, The Mad Trapper Snowshoe Series. This is a three race series, with each race offering 5 and 10km options. The focus of these events is on participation over competition and awards are distributed accordingly.

The start of the 2007 Canadian National Snowshoe Championships
at the Ark

We have just wrapped up our 6th season of Mad Trapper racing with the series continually showing annual growth. The Mad Trapper is now primarily sponsored by the Atlas Snowshoe Company, Solefit Orthotics, Bushtukah Great Outdoor Gear and Raid the North Adventure Racing.

In 2007, we started using the Mad Trapper as a vehicle to bring attention to the environment and global warming. This year participants were rewarded for carpooling to the events and for bringing their own non-disposable cups, plates and utensils. Following each race, a tour of the Ark is given and the essentials for living "off the grid" are explained.

Additionally in 2006, the 5 Peaks Trail Running Series began holding one of their races here at the Ark in the summer. Using the same trails as the Mad Trapper, these races also offer 5 and 10k options and also prioritize participation over competition.

This upcoming summer there has been talk about hosting a full weekend of off-road running races. We're thinking about calling it "Trailfest" or "Trailstock", and offering a few other off-the-wall races in addition to the main 5 Peaks event. We'll probably offer a race through a swamp, relay events, and a sprint race straight to the top of the mountain!

Should be fun...

Information on all of these events can be found at www.synergyark.com and www.5peaks.com.

Youth Programs

For the past 3 years we have hosted high school outdoor education programs and assisted them with their camping experiences. Using the campground and outhouses I built for the CFB Petawawa weeklong retreat, the kids are able to camp right on the grounds and be self sufficient for their meals. While here, the students participate in map and compass navigation sessions, high rope cliff rappelling, night hikes, team building activities, canoeing and general camp activities.

Preparing breakfast on Day 2 of a six day canoe trip in the
la Verendrye Wildlife Reserve

This year, Corporate Synergy is launching COLTT –
Canadian Outdoor Leadership Training for Teens. This is a
two week long program for a maximum of 12 teenagers
aged 14-18. The first week will be spent at the Ark
campground learning the same skills experienced by the
high school students. In the second week, participants will
be able to put all these new skills to the test during a five
day canoe trip in the la Verendrye Wildlife Reserve which is
just 2 hours north of the Ark.

Again, full information can be found at
www.synergyark.com.

Recommended Reading

Armstrong, Lance (2001). <u>It's Not About the Bike.</u> Berkely Trade: 304 pages

Byrne, Rhonda (2006). <u>The Secret.</u> Atria Books/Beyond Words: 198 pages

Canfield, Jack (2001). <u>Chicken Soup for the Soul.</u> HCI: 480 pages

Covey, Stephen R. (1989) <u>The 7 Habits of Highly Effective People.</u> Simon & Schuster: 358 pages

Fannin, Jim (2005) <u>S.C.O.R.E. for Life: The Five Keys to Optimum Achievement.</u> Harper-Collins Publishers: 183 pages

Hosseini, Khaled. (2003). <u>The Kite Runner.</u> Anchor Division, Random House: 394 pages

Kirshenbaum, Mira (2003). <u>The Emotional Energy Factor.</u> Bantam Dell: 266 pages

Thompson, Frank G. (1981). <u>Success is an Inside Job.</u> Diliton Publications Inc.: 188 pages

Tracy, Brian. (2003). <u>Goals: How to get everything you want – faster than you ever thought possible.</u> Berret-Koehler Publishers Inc.:290 pages

Westen, Robin. (2005). <u>Oprah Winfrey: I don't believe in failure.</u> Enslow Publishers: 128 pages

Zahab, Ray. (2007). <u>Running for my life.</u> Insomniac Press: 248 pages

ISBN 1425165265-5

Made in the USA
Monee, IL
11 January 2022

88690800R00115